THE CAIN & ABEL Syndrome

THE CAIN & ABEL Syndrome

Randy Carlson

A JANET THOMA BOOK

THOMAS NELSON PUBLISHERS
Nashville

Randy Carlson is available to speak at seminars on family related topics. He is also available for business consulting. To find out more about Mr. Carlson's availability please write or call:

Randy Carlson, M.A.
P.O. Box 37,000
Tucson, AZ 85740
(602) 742-6976

Published in Nashville, Tennessee, by Thomas Nelson, Inc., Publishers, and distributed in Canada by Word Communications, Ltd., Richmond, British Columbia, and in the United Kingdom by Word (UK), Ltd., Milton Keynes, England.

Scripture quotations are from the NEW KING JAMES VERSION of the Bible. Copyright © 1979, 1980, 1982, Thomas Nelson, Inc., Publishers. Quotations indicated KJV are from the King James Version.

Printed in the United States of America
94 95 96 97 98 99 -- 8 7 6 5 4 3 2

Library of Congress Cataloging-in-Publication Data

Carlson, Randy, 1951-
    The Cain and Abel syndrome / Randy Carlson.
        p.   cm.
    ISBN 0-8407-7719-1
    1. Sibling rivalry.   2. Brothers and sisters.   3. Adulthood—Psychological aspects.   I. Title.
    BF723.S43C37   1994
    158'.24—dc20   93-41878
                                                                CIP

ACKNOWLEDGMENTS

I would like to thank my brothers, Warren and Larry, for their support and encouragement during the writing of this manuscript and during our growing up years.

Special love and affection go to my wife, Donna, and our three children, Evan, Andrea, and Derek (DJ), for their patience with me during those times that this project distracted me from the family.

And to Fritz Ridenour, thank you for helping make this book a success.

To Warren and Larry, my big brothers, who have not only given me their cordial permission to share our sibling struggles and triumphs, but who, through the process of writing this book, have reminded me anew of the tremendous impact siblings have on each other. Thanks, guys. Without you I never could have become me!

CONTENTS

Part 1

DO BROTHERS AND SISTERS EVER GROW UP?

(the origins of the Cain and Abel syndrome)

Chapter 1

DOES RIVALRY REALLY MATTER?

"Mom always loved you best!"

If you're over thirty-five, you probably have no trouble associating this often-quoted line with the Smothers Brothers, whose popular television comedy show kept audiences in stitches for years. While their comedic Cain-and-Abel routine "turned sibling rivalry into an art form,"[1] neither Tommy nor Dick will admit to being jealous of each other in real life. In fact, their mom apparently loved Tommy, Dicky, and their sister, Sherry, equally. At the height of their popularity, their mother was often a member of the audience and would be asked by her sons to stand and take a bow.

But just because jealousy was never a problem for the Smothers Brothers, that doesn't mean their relationship was nothing but warm fuzzies. On the contrary, Tom says they find each other "totally irritating. Every year we have a kind of agreement to dissolve it all."

Dick agrees. In fact, he credits one of their squabbles with his getting together with his wife, Lorraine. Before doing one of their shows, he recalls, he and Tom had another fight and didn't give a particularly good performance. Afterward, a girl that Dick had met briefly a year earlier came backstage and asked him to go out with her and her friends. At first Dick wanted to turn her down, but then he thought about Tom and realized, *I don't want to go back to the hotel with THAT guy.* So he went out with the girl. It was practically a case of love at first sight, and a year later they were married.[2]

But while the Smothers Brothers fight, they are equally quick to forgive. As much as he loves his wife, Lorraine, Dick says, "What I have with Tommy is a prior commitment. This is my brother from the day I was born . . . he knows everything about me. Lorraine has to accept that." And Tommy adds, "He might not be the brother I would have picked at a certain point, but often the things we don't have choices about are the most significant in our lives. The things we can't control are the things that define us with each other."[3]

A LIFETIME CONNECTION

Not everyone who has siblings, or sibs, will identify with the "Mom-always-loved-you-best" complaint that Tommy made famous. While parental favoritism is a big bone of contention with many siblings, there is a lot more to sibling rivalry than that one issue. But what the Smothers Brothers say about each other and their real-life relationship does apply to everyone who has a brother or sister somewhere on this planet. Siblings do have "a prior commitment" with each other. We might not have picked our brothers and sisters if we had had the choice, but it's still true: The things we can't control are the things that define us with each other.

As a marriage and family therapist, I have become increasingly interested in what my clients think of their sibling relationships. As I began my research, my first question was, "Does anybody really care?" That is, when siblings are adults, do they even think about maintaining strong relationships with each other, or are they too busy with their own lives, their own families?

While co-hosting "Parent Talk," the daily radio call-in show I do with my colleague, Dr. Kevin Leman, I often conduct a little research over the air. One day I asked listeners to call in with any observations or stories they might have about their adult siblings. One caller asked the probing question, "Why do I want to invest time in improving my so-so relationship with my brother? Besides, we seldom see each other anyway."

Then another caller asked what was possibly an even more provocative question: "Are sibling relationships as important to maintain as your marriage?"

As I thought through the answer to the second question, I found the answer to the first. When a man and woman unite in marriage, they make vows of commitment to remain true to each other. One's first priority, then, must be one's marriage and any offspring that come from that union (which creates a whole new set of sibling relationships). As important as marriage is, however, it does not discount the importance and impact of sibling relationships, which, in a very real sense, are far more permanent than marriage relationships.

It is an unfortunate fact that marriage vows do get broken. As I do marriage counseling, my first goal is saving the marriage if at all possible, but human weakness and sin being what they are, commitments often crumble. It is possible to desert a spouse, drop a friend, or quit a job, but it is impossible to cut the powerful and lasting ties between siblings. In seminars I often point out:

**You can divorce a spouse,
but you cannot divorce your siblings.**

Your siblings are there for life. They were a part of you as you grew up, and they will remain a part of you until you die. You may see your siblings often or hardly at all. Your relationship may be friendly, indifferent, or even hostile, but whatever your situation, the effect of your siblings on your life—past, present and future—cannot be denied.

The sibling bond is a unique relationship. The history I have with my two older brothers, Warren and Larry, is different from anyone else's family history. I am connected to them in ways that I am not connected to my wife, Donna. Who I am today is a direct result of growing up with my siblings. I have been shaped by all the butting of heads, the bruises, the rejections, the acceptance, the laughter, and the tears that I shared with my brothers.

In her exhaustive study of siblings, *Mixed Feelings,* Francine Klagsbrun observes that "there is a certain kind of laughing, of crying, of knowing, that exists with a sibling that does not exist with anybody else in the world."[4] This "knowing" begins very early. As Klagsbrun points out, siblings become experts in knowing what the other is thinking and feeling. Toddlers ages two to three are often able to tell Mom or Dad what their baby sister or brother's expressions or noises mean when the parents don't understand at all. The older child will know instinctively that the baby is hungry or wants to be picked up, and almost always he or she is right. As siblings grow together, Klagsbrun says, they develop

a compelling need to accumulate the knowledge they have of each other. Each wants to know what makes the other tick. Each wants to know which buttons to push to make the other cry or cringe. Each also wants to know how to make the other laugh and how to win the other's love and approval. In its intensity, their mutual knowledge becomes all-embracing—a naked understanding that encompasses the very essence of the other's being.

Once gained, that gut understanding remains a crucial part of the link between siblings for life. Even after years of separation, an adult brother or sister may quickly, intuitively, pick up on another's thoughts, sympathize with the other's needs, or zero in—unerringly—on the other's insecurities.[5]

Siblings' Unresolved Problems

In doing research for this book, I have talked to and surveyed thousands of people regarding the sibling relationship, and I have learned that people do care—very much—about their brothers and sisters. In seminars I ask the question, "How many of you would like to improve your relationship with your siblings?" Many in the audience nod, and a few even groan as they realize their relationship to a brother or sister (or possibly both) is not what it should or could be.

Some of the remarks on their questionnaires have included:

- "Why can't we just be friends?"
- "I wish we had known each other better."
- "Why does my older brother still think I can't do anything right?"
- "What keeps my sister so far away, so distant in thought and emotions?"
- "Doing this questionnaire has brought tears to my eyes."

In the surveys I have taken, 97 percent of those responding reported that a very good or somewhat good sibling relationship is important, and 93 percent said they expected their children to grow up and get along with their siblings. Even more significantly, 91 percent of those surveyed wanted to improve their adult sibling relationships to some degree.

But along with all this affirmation of the sibling relationship 63 percent reported "unresolved issues" between themselves and at least one other adult sibling. And as I went through the questionnaires, it became obvious that this figure should probably be even higher because some respondents refused to admit unresolved issues. They said they simply had a "disagreement" or "misunderstanding." From my research with siblings of all ages, I think it's safe to say that at least 75 percent of all adult siblings have questions, issues, or problems with at least one other sibling, many of which have never been discussed or worked through.

A BROADER DEFINITION OF SIBLING RIVALRY

As moms and dads from across the nation call us on "Parent Talk," their number-one complaint centers on fighting and bickering between their young children. When children don't get along, we have no trouble labeling that as "sibling rivalry." The dictionary defines a *rival* as "a person who attempts to equal or surpass another or pursues the same object as another; a competitor."[6] Children certainly fit this description. Instead of an "abundance mentality," which believes there is plenty of whatever we need to go around, most children operate on the "scarcity mentality," a belief that "there's not enough of what I want to go around." And that includes love or attention from their parents.

You probably see the scarcity mentality operating among your children, as Donna and I do among ours. If we pay attention to D.J., our youngest, somehow or other we have taken away from Andrea or Evan, D.J.'s older siblings, and they let us know that in subtle or not so subtle ways. Or if we allow Evan to do something special because he's the oldest, Andrea or D.J. loudly protests, "That's not fair!"

Does the scarcity mentality vanish as children grow into adulthood? Hardly. The principle still operates but it's much more subtle. For many adult siblings there is still not enough love, attention, or whatever it is they need. In their minds, a brother or a sister is still hogging the limelight, controlling the situation, or getting more attention from parents or others in the family.

But adults are not ready to admit even to themselves that they have a scarcity mentality. We see this in how they refer to not being on the best of terms with another adult sibling. Instead of calling it "sibling rivalry," they say they are "estranged" or there is "competition," or perhaps it gets labeled "a strange relationship."

One of the first questions I use to survey adults about their sibling relationships asks, "Do you experience adult sibling rivalry?" One thirty-four-year-old woman replied, "Not exactly rivalry—differences of opinions and lifestyles."

On the back of that same questionnaire I also asked, "If you were to write a letter to your adult sibling, sharing your own feelings of concern or delight with your relationship, what would you write?" This same woman shared what she would write to a sister two and a half years younger:

I don't care how many degrees your husband has. I don't care that he makes as much in a month as my husband does in a year. We weren't raised to count our material goods. Get your nose out of the air and get real! We love you and your husband for who you are, not what you're worth dollar-wise.

Most of us don't put it quite so fervently, but we say the same thing. Whenever we feel dislike or indifference for a brother or sister, we say it's his

We don't really see any rivalry on our part. It's our sibling who "wants to compete."

or her fault, just as we did when we were kids. That is, we don't really see any rivalry on *our* part. It's *our sibling* who "wants to compete" or "who doesn't care" or "who never calls."

The more I researched adult sibling relationships, the more I saw the need for a broader definition of sibling rivalry. Here's what I came up with:

Any situation where brothers and sisters, who are now grown and usually have families of their own are *still attempting to equal or surpass one another in some way.* For reasons easy or difficult to identify, they don't get along with each other as well as they wish they could.

As Jane Greer observes in *Adult Sibling Rivalry*, sibling rivalry originates in childhood, but it goes far beyond. She writes: "Its legacies are numerous and powerful, and they often linger for decades . . . precisely because these legacies run so far back—for many people, all the way to birth—they have an extraordinary grip on our thoughts, emotions, and behaviors: in short, on who we are."[7]

SEARCHING FOR ANSWERS TO THE RIVALRY RIDDLE

Adult sibling rivalry covers a broad spectrum. At one end are adult siblings who just don't have that much time for each other and seldom communicate. ("We live at different ends of the country and we have our own lives so we've just drifted apart.") At the other end of the spectrum is adult sibling rivalry that becomes open hostility and even violent. ("We probably couldn't spend more than ten minutes together in the same room.")

As the youngest of three brothers, my own sibling rivalry issues fall somewhere between these two extremes. Nonetheless, I have always desired closer relationships with my brothers. This is not to say that we argue, fight, or just ignore one another. Far from it. We get along very well—at a certain level. But we've never gone any deeper than that, and I have wondered why. This has sent me searching for ways to make our relationship better. So, in part, this book is a description of my own pilgrimage as a sibling and what I've learned firsthand about trying to solve the "rivalry riddle."

As I grew up, my brothers were so much older—eleven and five years my senior—that they tended to ignore me. We all lived in the same house, but their worlds were far different from mine. Except for teasing me now and then because they thought I was such a "little pest," they left me out of their activities, not exactly by design but simply because I was too young to fit into their plans in the first place.

A rule of counseling is that the patterns of childhood continue to repeat themselves when we become adults. Because I've always wanted the approval and respect of my brothers, it often happens that little things, minor incidents that shouldn't really matter, turn out to matter a great deal to me.

I believe siblings expect their brothers and sisters to respect them, to accept them, and to do the right thing every time. Unfortunately, siblings with these expectations are frequently doomed to disappointment. I have seen it happen so often that I have developed an equation to describe the cycle:

$$E - R = D$$
(Expectations minus reality equals disappointment.)

In talking with many adult siblings, I see this equation operating again and again. One sibling has certain expectations of another ("He should *understand*. After all, he's my brother!"), then has to face reality and settle for a lot less—a minus, if you please. The result is disappointment and one sibling's feeling that the other one is wrong.

It is, of course, our *expectations* that betray us. Stephen Covey uses an imaginary map to describe the difference between expectations and reality. This map, which we have fixed in our minds, depicts what *should* be, not what actually is. Writes Covey, "a lot of people think

their maps are accurate and that 'this is the way it really is'— your map is wrong."[8]

Covey's analogy dovetails nicely with the formula "expectations minus reality equals disappointment." I see this formula frequently at work in my own life, particularly in regard to my expectations of my brother Larry. I expect him to do one thing (my map), but he often does another (his map). Because I perceive that my map is accurate and his is wrong, I find myself being disappointed. It has happened all our lives and recently, during a visit by Larry and his wife, it happened again.

THE CASE OF THE MISSING BOARD MEMBER

As Larry and I reached adulthood, our career paths took different directions, but due to geography they continue to cross on a regular basis. Today I am president of "Today's Family Life" and "Parent Talk," two radio ministries associated with the Family Life Broadcasting System, which has seven radio stations in Michigan, New Mexico, and Arizona. Its national headquarters is in Tucson, where I live with my family.

Larry is president of Youth Haven Ranch, an organization he co-founded in 1967 with our parents, Morry and Dorothy Carlson, to minister to disadvantaged and underprivileged children from the inner city. A college student when the ranch was started, Larry was involved from the very beginning and had much to do with getting its various programs underway.

The first Youth Haven Ranch, located near Lansing, Michigan, still remains the national headquarters. Larry makes his home on the ranch property and spends most of the year administrating Youth Haven Ministries from there. Every now and then, however, he will come to Arizona to visit the western branch of the Youth Haven ministry, "the desert ranch" located between Tucson and Phoenix.

On one such trip, Larry and his wife, Cheri, flew into Phoenix, where he had business appointments. I had known he was coming and had called the Youth Haven offices in Michigan to see if he could do me a favor and attend a meeting of our board of directors. (I serve on Larry's Youth Haven Ranch board, and he serves on the board of Family Life Broadcasting System; we try to get to each other's meetings as often as we can.)

Larry wasn't in, but I talked to his secretary and said, "We're having a special meeting concerning 'Today's Family Life' on Wednesday around 2:00 P.M. It would be great if Larry could drive down from Phoenix for that meeting. We could use his input, but, of course, if he's busy, I'll understand."

"I'll see that Larry gets the message," she replied, and I hung up, assuming Larry would come unless he notified me otherwise.

My Wednesday board meeting came and went and Larry did not appear, which disappointed me a great deal. Later in the week, he and Cheri drove down to visit my parents, who in recent years have been spending the winter months in Tucson due to my father's poor health.

While in town, Larry and Cheri dropped by to see Donna and me, but during their rather brief visit Larry seemed preoccupied, almost "on the edge of his chair," wanting to get going. I chose not to mention Larry's absence from the board meeting, and he never mentioned it either. Before Larry and Cheri left, we talked about trying to get together again sometime that week but it never happened, and the day of their departure arrived. They were staying in a motel next door to our "Today's Family Life" offices. Indeed, I could literally look out my office window and see Larry and Cheri loading their rental car for the drive back to the airport in Phoenix.

Surely he'll come over and say good-bye, I thought to myself as I worked on some reports. Finally, Cheri came up to the office to tell me it had been nice seeing us and she wished their stay could have been longer. We chatted cordially for a while, then she left. A few minutes later I looked out the window and saw their car pulling out of the motel parking lot. Larry had not dropped by to say good-bye, and mixed with my irritation and anger were feelings that this had all happened before. Once again I had been ignored by an older brother who was too busy to give me five minutes of his time.

As a mature adult, I should have been willing to go down to Larry's motel room to bid him good-bye, but after all, he was the visitor. The least he could have done was to come up to my office to tell me it had been a great week and that he hoped we could get together soon. Instead, as I had often done all my life, I perceived that Larry had his own agenda that he was pursuing without paying respects to his little brother.

As I looked back on the entire week and the disappointments I felt because Larry hadn't fulfilled my expectations, I saw a picture of our sibling relationship all our lives. On several occasions I had been left feeling rejected and unrespected. One of them occurred in an alley near our house when I was around five and ten-year-old Larry was leaving to go somewhere with one of his friends.

I wanted to tag along, but Larry snapped, "Get out of here . . . get lost!" And then he and his friend ran down the alley, leaving me, "the baby of the family," behind.

There is nothing exceptional about this little story. Almost all younger brothers and sisters can remember times that older siblings tried to ditch them or told them to "get lost." But as I pointed out in *Unlocking the Secrets of Your Childhood Memories,* the secret to anyone's outlook on life is hidden within his or her earliest recollections. There is a "law of creative consistency" that says, "People remember only those events from early childhood that are consistent with their present view of themselves and the world around them."[9]

As I sort through my memories of Larry and my other older brother, Warren, I come up with negative pictures more often than not. Because they were both so much older than I, neither one of them had any time for me; they had their own interests and schedules. My memories of them almost always involve being left out, being told to "scram!" or just being ignored. Some of the most vivid examples revolved around our family hobby when we were kids—ham radio.

Warren got into it first when he used to hang around a neighbor who had a ham set. He soon had his own equipment and then Larry decided he'd be a ham operator too.

When I was around seven or eight, I'd listen longingly at the door of Warren's room as my older brothers talked on their ham radio sets. I was fascinated as I heard their conversations with people hundreds and even thousands of miles away, but even more impressive was their role in tracking tornadoes. Because we lived in the Midwest, tornadoes were always a threat. Whenever there was a tornado alert, Larry and Warren would be called down to Civil Defense headquarters to run ham radio sets and pick up reports from the spotters watching for the approach of any ominous, black funnel clouds.

I was too young to go along, of course, and I would have to watch them get in Warren's '57 Ford and head off into the darkness to be heroes while I remained behind feeling left out of all the excitement. Helping protect our town from the danger of tornadoes seemed to me the height of being important and worthwhile, and I wondered how I could ever get into the exclusive ham radio club.

Larry did let me talk to people now and then on his ham set, but all I got to do was ask questions like "How is the weather?" and little else. Like Warren, he was deep into his own interests and schedule, and he didn't have time to show his little brother how it all worked. I was in sixth grade when I finally got into ham radio, but it wasn't through Larry or Warren. As so often was the case, I had to find my own way because my brothers weren't there for me.

Despite the fact that I have a marriage-and-family-therapist shingle hanging on my office wall, I have to admit that at times I still struggle with feelings of insecurity that began way back there when I was "the little twerp" of the family. As I trailed my big brothers through life, it seemed that much of the time they didn't just ignore me; as I interpreted it, they discounted me. Even today that remains a hot button that Larry, in particular, can press without even trying, as the "no good-bye" incident proves. All this is childish, of course, and I am the first to admit it. I often ask myself, *Why is that hot button still there after all these years? Why can't I just grow up, become a man, and put away these childish things?*

But of course, putting away such childish things is not that simple, nor is it done in an instant, not even by a professional counselor. As the co-authors of a counseling textbook put it:

It may be that some extraordinary people (like saints) do not carry their childish attitudes over into their adult lives, but the rest of us harbor a child within us all our lives long. . . . So far as that child's relations with siblings are concerned, early attitudes and beliefs are long-enduring.[10]

Indeed they are. In fact, these attitudes and beliefs last a lifetime. You see, the person you are today has more to do with the interaction that went on between you and your siblings as you all grew up together than what schools you went to, the jobs you've held, or even whom you've married. As Jane Greer cogently observes:

> Moreover, what you experienced in relation to your siblings still affects your perception of who you are, what you want, and how you see the world. Even if your direct interaction with your siblings ceased when you became an adult, the time you spent with them has changed you forever. More than that: it has *shaped* you. . . . Siblinghood is one of the fundamental formative aspects of your life.[11]

How Satisfying Are Your Sibling Relationships?

To assess where you stand with your siblings today, take the Sibling Satisfaction Quiz below. Check yes or no to the following statements to help reveal how warm or cool you perceive your relationship to be. Then add comments to explain your answer. Note that each question provides spaces for evaluating relationships with two siblings. If you have more than that, just add information in the margin or on a small piece of paper that you can clip to this page. Be sure to put down any comments that occur to you as you apply these statements to your siblings. What you say could be very revealing about how you really feel.

Sibling Satisfaction Quiz

1. I enjoy spending time with my sibling.
   Sibling 1 (name _____): __Yes __No
   Comments: _____
   Sibling 2 (name _____): __Yes __No
   Comments: _____

2. I can share openly with my sibling.
   Sibling 1 (name _____): __Yes __No
   Comments: _____

   Sibling 2 (name _____): __Yes __No
   Comments: _____

3. I feel understood by my sibling.
   Sibling 1 (name _____): __Yes __No
   Comments: _____

   Sibling 2 (name _____): __Yes __No
   Comments: _____

4. My sibling respects me.
   Sibling 1 (name _____): __Yes __No
   Comments: _____

   Sibling 2 (name _____): __Yes __No
   Comments: _____

5. I respect my sibling.
   Sibling 1 (name _____): __Yes __No
   Comments: _____

   Sibling 2 (name _____): __Yes __No
   Comments: _____

6. If I were in trouble, my sibling would be there for me.
   Sibling 1 (name _____): __Yes __No
   Comments: _____

   Sibling 2 (name _____): __Yes __No
   Comments: _____

7. I want my sibling's input in my life.
   Sibling 1 (name _____): __Yes __No
   Comments: _____

   Sibling 2 (name _____): __Yes __No
   Comments: _____

How did you do? Did you target any relationships that need work? If you are typical, you may have discovered that your relationship with at least one sibling is not all it could be. Why is this the case? There may be several reasons, and they can all be traced back to one basic problem that causes more friction between siblings than any other. We'll look at that problem in Chapter 2.

WHAT THIS BOOK CAN DO FOR YOU AND YOUR SIBLINGS

This book will give you insights into what happened in your family "way back when" and how it shaped who you are today. You will also find help to:

- Be able to live and work together with your siblings more happily and effectively (especially if they live in close proximity to you).
- Resolve old issues that still affect you and your siblings and the rest of your family today.
- Assuage guilt you may feel over a poor sibling relationship. (This is particularly true if you have been stringently taught the importance of "loving one another.")
- Break any dysfunctional cycles that have led to estrangement with your siblings. You will be able to rear your own children better and help them avoid the negative effects of severe sibling rivalry.
- Know yourself better and learn why you are the way you are. Your siblings have had an awful lot to do with that.

In fact, your sibling relationships have had as much to do with how you are today as your relationship with your parents. In short, the better you understand your siblings, the better you will understand yourself and how the Cain and Abel syndrome impacts all of you.

Your sibling relationships have had as much to do with how you are today as your relationship with your parents.

Chapter 2

THE CAIN AND ABEL SYNDROME

Most siblings will say they want better relationships with their brothers and sisters. However, it is a fact of life that most of our energies are directed to other relationships—with our own children and spouses or those related to our work, our church, or our community activities. Meanwhile, adult sibling relationships often are ignored, neglected, or at least minimized. Busy with our own lives, we bury our feelings regarding our siblings, but in so doing we ignore a crucial truth:

**When we bury our emotions,
we bury them alive.**

Pressures produced by poor sibling relationships, even those we may think have long been forgotten over the years, can build within us and become a veritable Mount Saint Helens waiting to erupt. When adult siblings come together in tense or stressful situations, what often happens is what I call "the sibling moment." The pressure becomes too great as adult siblings revert to their childhood roles, and an explosion occurs.

Peggy, the second oldest in a family of six children, shared a story that vividly demonstrates how this can happen. Last year Peggy's father died suddenly, and three weeks later her mother was diagnosed with leukemia. The mother lasted six weeks, and during that time Peggy and her five siblings all moved in to help and be a part of Mom's last days. Not surprisingly, the stress and tension mounted and old sibling rivalries came to the surface. Peggy described what happened this way:

Pressures produced by poor sibling relationships, . . . can build within us and become a veritable Mount Saint Helens waiting to erupt.

"We had six adult kids living under the same roof, and then with the tension of our mom dying right after our father, things kind of hit a head the day after Mom's death. A couple of my brothers got into a major argument, including a fistfight, and I tried to step between them. The fight continued and got so bad that when one brother left the house, the other one stormed after him and slammed the back door so hard he literally broke it off its hinges. We had to replace that door before the funeral."

Although tempers cooled and the six siblings got through the funeral, there wasn't much speaking to one another and tensions have continued on and off ever since.

It's easy to think that perhaps the stress of having two parents die caused the blowup, but I doubt it. Their deaths only brought out what was already in the stew. Buried emotions caused the fistfight, and these feelings continue to generate tensions among Peggy and her siblings today.

When Peggy's brothers got into a knock-down-drag-out brawl the day after their mother died, a sibling moment wreaked chaos on the already-shattered family. Such "moments" are nothing new—not for this family or for families throughout the history of mankind. The first sibling rivals, Cain and Abel, can attest to that.

How the "Cain and Abel Syndrome" Began

One of the most vivid examples of the ultimate "Mount Saint Helens" eruption between siblings is the biblical account of Cain and Abel. Sibling rivalry, fueled by jealousy and hatred, exploded into a murderous sibling moment that resulted in Cain's killing his younger brother.

Why was Cain so murderously jealous of Abel? The account in Genesis 4 tells us that Abel, a sheepherder, brought a more acceptable sacrifice to God than did Cain, a farmer. God accepted Abel's sacrifice but rejected Cain's.

As we picture this sibling scenario, it will help to try to understand how Cain felt. Here he was, first-born in the family—actually the first-born in history. He was supposed to be the leader and the pacesetter for his little brother, but what happened? Little brother showed him up in history's first example of the second-born displacing the first-born. Abel took over and became the approved and righteous one among Adam and Eve's offspring. Some Bible scholars even speculate that by bringing an offering that God had to refuse, Cain lost his birthright.[1]

While we cannot be absolutely sure Cain really thought he had lost his birthright, there is no question that he had lost face and a lot of the honor. Jealousy burned deep in Cain's heart, and he plotted his revenge.

Because Cain was his brother, Abel wasn't at all suspicious when his big brother invited him to go for a walk and have a little chat. Who knows? Perhaps Cain told Abel he wanted to learn some secrets about how to do a better job. At any rate, Cain got his baby brother out into a field where Mom and Dad couldn't hear his cries—and killed him. Sibling rivalry had sunk to its lowest depths.

An Ancient Syndrome, Still Present

While Cain was the first sibling to slay a brother or sister, he certainly wasn't the last. The Cain and Abel syndrome has been with us throughout history, and in a sense it is part of every sibling relationship.

A *syndrome* is a group of signs and symptoms that collectively indicate or characterize a disease or some other problem. The Cain and Abel syndrome includes competition, jealousy, anger, fear, and sometimes even hatred and murder. Obviously, not all siblings resort to murder (although many of them might think about it at times). The point is, however, those same basic raw emotions of jealousy, resentment, ill will, spite, insecurity, and paranoia are still part of sibling relationships today to one degree or another.

One of the key characteristics of a dysfunctional family is that within it a pattern of behavior is repeated over and over again. When Cain killed Abel, he didn't commit the first sin in the Bible. His parents, Adam and Eve, had already done that, and with it they started a dysfunctional chain reaction of pride, jealousy, disobedience, lying, and even violence that has been passed down through the generations.

The term *dysfunctional family* began as a buzzword in the eighties and is now standard counseling vocabulary in the nineties. There are various definitions of *dysfunctional*, particularly in books that focus on co-dependency and addiction. For example, John Bradshaw, whose television programs and books on the family are well known, defines a dysfunctional family as one in which there is denial and delusion as well as a lack of freedom and intimacy that results in family members not being able to have their individual needs met.[2]

A simple illustration I use to describe what it means to be dysfunctional is a wristwatch that may work well only part of the time. One day it may keep perfect time, and the next day it will run slow or fast. Such a watch is dysfunctional; sometimes it works and does what it was created to do, but other times it has problems. Just as a dysfunctional watch does not keep perfect time, a dysfunctional family does not have perfect relationships, nor does it nurture everyone in the family completely in every situation.

There are degrees of dysfunction in all families because, by definition, a dysfunctional family is one in which there are imperfect people trying to function perfectly but not always succeeding. Sometimes this can get very serious and very sick. Alcoholism, incest, child abuse, spouse abuse, and any number of other horrors can be present in a dysfunctional family. But so-called "normal" families have their dysfunctional moments too. Certainly, sibling rivalry is part of the dysfunctional cycle, but that cycle *can* be broken. The Cain and Abel syndrome is a potential danger to any sibling relationship, but brothers and sisters are not automatically doomed to a lifetime of rivalry and estrangement operating under the views of Sigmund Freud. According to Jane Leder in *Brothers and Sisters: How They Shape Our Lives*,

> Jealous rivalry for parental love and attention dominated Freud's evaluation of the sibling relationship. He emphasized intensity and ruthlessness of the child's hostility to his siblings. . . . Freud postulated that children can much more easily allow themselves to hate a sibling than hate a parent on whom they are completely dependent.[3]

Freud's ideas were heavily influenced by his own hostile and disparaging relationships with his five sisters. He also had trouble dealing with a baby brother born when Freud was very young. Freud viewed little Julius as an unwanted intruder whom he disliked so much that at times he even thought about murdering him. Julius's death only nine months later caused feelings of guilt and self-reproach that plagued Freud throughout his life. The only sibling with whom Freud got along well was his brother, Alexander, ten years younger, who was his constant admirer and who obeyed Freud's every wish.[4]

Freud was correct in observing the natural inclination toward rivalry among siblings. It is true that in all of us lie the seeds of the Cain and Abel syndrome, which, if left to sprout and grow unchallenged can cause life-long problems. But Freud's contentions that intense sibling rivalry is inevitable overstated the case to such a degree that he seemed unable to recognize any possibilities of real affection between siblings. As we shall see in a later chapter, siblings *can* achieve unusually high degrees of trust and intimacy.

If you want to improve your relationship with that sibling who never calls or perhaps calls too often and drives you a little crazy, the first step is to sort out the same choices that were given to Cain: succumb to pride, jealousy, or competitiveness (what we are often prone to call "hurt feelings") or cultivate right attitudes of love, faith, and long-suffering—perhaps a great deal of long-suffering, as the stories on the following pages will demonstrate.

IDENTIFYING THE CAIN AND ABEL SYNDROME

To see if the Cain and Abel syndrome is affecting you and your siblings, check to see if any of the following characteristics are present *to any degree* in your relationships. Don't rationalize about whose fault it is. Just identify anything that may be coming between you and your siblings.

_____ Jealousy		_____ Hostility
_____ Anger		_____ Secretiveness
_____ Resentment		_____ Childishness
_____ Competition		_____ Ill will
_____ Violence		_____ Unforgiveness
_____ Distrust		_____ Bitterness
_____ Manipulation		_____ Paranoia
_____ Pettiness		_____ Indifference

If any of the above characteristics are present in your relationship to another sibling, you are being affected by the Cain and Abel syndrome. You can, however, weaken its grip and even escape completely from it if you are willing to make the effort.

As you read further in this book, I hope you will not only think about your own sibling relationships but also become much more aware of what is happening as you rear your own children. Anything you can do to negate the effect of the Cain

Right now your children are deciding the kind of relationship they will have twenty, thirty, and forty years in the future.

and Abel syndrome on your own family is of vital importance. Right now your children are deciding the kind of relationship they will have twenty, thirty, and forty years in the future.

While rivalry between siblings is natural, there are ways to control it or at least not encourage it unwittingly. We will look more closely at how to raise kids with as little rivalry as possible in Part 3 of this book.

WHAT MANY SIBLINGS GO WITHOUT

As adult siblings speak of their experience with the Cain and Abel syndrome, I hear a great deal about a problem exemplified by that simple line made famous by Rodney Dangerfield: "I don't get no respect!"

For example, Denise called a "Parent Talk" show we did on siblings to share her frustrations after reaching out to her older sister to heal what she felt was at best a strained relationship. But the older sister flatly refused to close the gap that years of rivalry had caused when they were younger.

Instead of getting a warm welcome and perhaps some words of approval for being the one who took the first step, all Denise heard was "I'm not really interested." The same coolness she had often felt while trying to compete with her big sister, first for grades and later for dates, was still there.

The refusal of Denise's sister to reconcile or at least begin talking is one more example of how patterns that develop in childhood can continue into adult life. When I asked Denise what she had wanted from her older sister that she never got, she replied, "Respect. I feel as if she didn't respect me when we were kids, and she doesn't respect me now."

Due to strong differences in temperament and personality, some siblings are never able to understand and empathize with each other. The longer I talked with Denise, the clearer it became that this was her situation. When she and her older sister were young, they had never really bonded as siblings.

To use a radio broadcasting analogy, bonding means being on the same wavelength or frequency—able to receive each other's signals with empathy and understanding. When husbands and wives fail to bond the marriage is soon in trouble, and the first sign is a lack of respect for one another. The same is true of siblings.

For some first-born sibs, for example, the arrival of a younger child can be such a threat and source of insecurity, they never accept their sibling. One pair of researchers who specialize in observing young children frequently found families where it was usually the older child who consistently rejected a younger sibling, even though the younger child tried to be friends and do everything he or she could to please the older one.[5]

Denise seemed to fall into this category of younger siblings who, when asked about their adult brother or sister, say flatly, "We never got along."

LACK OF RESPECT AT ITS WORST

Lack of respect is a key symptom of the failure of siblings to bond as children, and they often remain at odds or in a state of enmity all their lives. At its very worst, lack of respect becomes abuse, and recent research has shown that children who are constantly picked on by their siblings can wind up with psychological problems, including high levels of anxiety, low self-esteem, and depression.

> *Lack of respect is a key symptom of the failure of siblings to bond as children.*

According to two studies conducted at the University of Michigan and reported at a meeting of the American Psychological Association, children squabble and even hit one another as they are growing up together, but when the relationship is one-sided, with one sibling getting the brunt of the punishment, it can cause serious problems. About one-fourth of the relationships studied were so bad parents should have stepped in, but they had done nothing even though they knew about the problem.

Sibling conflicts that get abusive are more common from ages six to twelve than during the teenage years. While one study focused on long-term physical conflicts, the second study was limited to people whose experience would have to be called abusive. These siblings were repeatedly beaten up, sexually abused, or emotionally abused by constantly being humiliated, ridiculed, or shamed.[6]

Recently I counseled a thirty-seven-year-old woman who had been repeatedly abused sexually by her brothers. They had used Bible verses (taken totally out of context) to prove that their behavior was acceptable and even to be expected. Only during the past year had she realized that all of this was not only sinful, but sick. While her story was hard to believe in light of all the awareness of sexual abuse that has developed in recent years, it illustrates the tremendous power siblings can hold over each other, even into adult life.

As part of her therapy and healing process, the woman had broken off relationships with her brothers. She was making progress but was still very traumatized by the cycle of abuse that had lasted for more than thirty years.

FOUR DISAPPOINTING BROTHERS

Lack of respect occurs in sibling relationships to different degrees. Often, older siblings take advantage of younger ones. That was the case for Mary Lou.

You would think that being born "the baby princess of the family" and having four big brothers would mean always enjoying lots of protection and respect, but for Mary Lou that didn't happen, particularly when their mother suffered a stroke and had to be put in a nursing home. Mary Lou and her four older brothers had all married by that time and the brothers were living in other states. They all got together and decided they would "help out financially" by sending fifty dollars a month each for some of the mother's support. After getting Mom settled, the brothers all went back to their respective homes and left Mary Lou in charge because she lived nearby with her own family.

That was three years ago. Since then, only one brother has lived up to his pledge of fifty dollars a month and the others almost totally ignore their mother as well as Mary Lou. During one Christmas holiday, the mother went into severe depression and sat in her chair, with drool running out of her mouth, just staring into space. In an attempt to bring her mother back to reality, Mary Lou went out and bought gifts and cards, addressing them to the mother as if they had been sent by her four sons. She took all the gifts and cards over to the nursing home and gave them to Mom and within an hour she was back to normal because she thought "the boys" had finally thought of her.

When Mary Lou told me her story, I explained that almost every family has one sibling who turns out to be the family

C.E.O., the "chief emotional officer." Obviously, Mary Lou had inherited this job. "It's like playing tag," I told her. "You're it, and you can never find your brothers to make them it."

"Well, they know now I sent Mom the presents. When I decided to do it, there wasn't time to contact them. If I hadn't done something to make her think her sons loved her, she would have had to go on medication."

"When you took the gifts to your mom, two things were happening," I explained. "First, you wanted to encourage your mother and make her feel better. That part was wonderful, but at the same time, you were encouraging irresponsibility on the part of your brothers. They need a good strong letter from you, telling them that you're going to be responsible for your relationship with your mother, but not theirs. You need to put the ball squarely in their court and let them take that responsibility."

It turned out that Mary Lou had already written that letter, and she shared it with me. She had sent a copy to each brother, telling him what had happened over Christmas and how uncomfortable it had made her feel when she had to cover for them. Her letter went on to say:

It's hard for me to tell you exactly how I am feeling. Ever since Mom had the stroke I have tried to cover the bases with little or no help from any of you. I'm angry because all the burden for her care seems to fall on me. I have enjoyed helping Mom in her times of need, but the burden has become too heavy. This must change. I cannot continue to fulfill your responsibilities. It's hurting me, it's hurting Mom, and you are hurting yourselves by neglecting her as you have. Mom needs you, I need you, and we need each other.

I feel that I am the only one who genuinely cares about Mom. It is hard to explain how hurt and angry and discouraged I am by what has been going on and by your lack of support and encouragement. From now on, I intend to be responsible only for my relationship to Mom. I expect you to become fully responsible for your relationship to Mom, as well as your part in supporting her financially and, above all, emotionally.

I want you all to know that writing this letter grieves me

very much. I love each of you and I pray for you, and I hope that soon our entire family will be willing to pull together instead of putting all the load on only one person.

Mary Lou's words are a good model for how to confront siblings who are not only showing disrespect for other family members but a total lack of care and concern. In many cases, erring siblings don't realize the impact of what they are doing or failing to do. Confronting them with an open charge of disrespect and lack of compassion should be done respectfully but with stark honesty. Mary Lou's letter does that, and it did change the situation, as I will explain later.

A TARGET FOR CONSTANT PUT-DOWNS

Earlier in this chapter I introduced the term *sibling moment* with a story about a family of six children and how two of them got into a knock-down-drag-out brawl during a sibling moment that involved their mother's death. Many sibling moments aren't as violent, but nonetheless they can be stressful and depressing. For example, when I talked with Norma, the baby of a family of four children, she wanted help with how to deal with her older siblings, particularly her two older sisters. She told me they made her the constant target of their put-downs whenever the family got together.

Whenever adult sibs get together, it becomes a sibling moment. There is a tendency to fall right back into the old patterns that were established years before during childhood. In Norma's case, her brother was fourteen years older than she was, one sister was twelve years older, and the second sister was six years older. I could relate to her story very well as she said, "They don't listen to me when I try to say something. Instead, they just shoot their darts, so to speak. They tell me I don't know this or I don't know that, so I tend not to say very much. I try not to be their target, but it's almost as if they want to put me down as a way of feeling better themselves. I don't want to return their put-downs, but I do want to be assertive and let them know it hurts."

"Have you ever confronted them about what they're doing?" I asked.

"I've tried talking to them, and they come back at me with both barrels. Now I'm finding out that I've got to break this cycle because my daughter is eight years old and my nephew—my sister's son—is ten, and he's doing the very same thing to her. If something doesn't happen, this whole thing is going to snowball."

I encouraged Norma by observing that she had a lot of insight about the situation but she needed to take an assertive course of action if anything were going to change. It's very hard for older siblings to give younger siblings a break and let them grow up. As Norma pointed out, it's almost as if they want to keep the younger siblings in their place in order to feel better about their own status.

When I urged Norma to become more assertive, she said she had been trying, but her sisters—who are obviously very verbal — were telling her that she was just being spoiled and wanting her own way. I explained to Norma that with siblings there is often a "mob psychology," particularly when they all get together. Roles have been set and lines have been drawn. When one sibling wants to change the rules of the game, the rest don't like it. In Norma's case, she is the baby and they want to keep her in that role. By letting her older siblings know that she is tired of being put down it's as if Norma is breaking the rules, and that isn't allowed.

I told Norma one idea might be sitting down, one-on-one, with her sisters and letting them know how she feels. If that fails to bring any results, she could just not get together as often with them. One other possibility would be writing a letter that would set some healthy limits, saying that her home was open, but the put-downs had to stop because her children were wondering why their aunts talked to their mother this way.

Whatever course Norma took, she had to decide on a way to confront her siblings firmly but caringly. In Chapter 8 we'll be looking at some specific ways to do this kind of confronting.

CHASING THAT ELUSIVE BRASS RING

Denise, Mary Lou, and Norma are typical examples of siblings who expected to receive respect, acceptance, and support from older siblings, but the realities of life set them up for disappointment. I know how they feel. As I grew up eleven and five years behind my brothers, it seemed I would always be looking up at them while they were looking ahead—to their plans, their activities, and their personal agendas, which seldom seemed to include me, or at least they didn't include me often enough.

And when we became adults, I continued to chase that elusive brass ring. But no matter how hard I tried to impress them and show them that I was more than the baby brother of the family, it seemed as if I always wound up feeling like Rodney Dangerfield, wondering if I'd ever be recognized as a true equal.

The incident when Larry left Tucson without saying good-bye has proved to be something of a turning point in my quest. In a later chapter, I'll describe how I confronted him about my feelings and how we achieved better levels of communication than we ever had before. Both of us now realize that we have engaged in childish behavior over the years, and we're both making progress on changing that.

The following quiz may help you uncover some childish attitudes and behavior that may still linger in your own adult sibling relationships. As you read each of the following statements, put checks or the appropriate sibling's initials under "Then" if the statement was true of you or your siblings during childhood. Do the same under "Now" if the statement is true to any degree in your adult sibling relationships.

Assessing Your Sibling Relationship

Then   Now

____   ____   I'm looking for approval from my sibling.
____   ____   My sibling is looking for my approval.
____   ____   Resolving conflicts is difficult.
____   ____   Mom or Dad get involved with our disputes.
____   ____   There is competition between us.
____   ____   My sibling reacts in petty ways to things I say or do.
____   ____   My sibling holds grudges.
____   ____   My sibling won't just come out and tell me how he or she is feeling.

_____   _____   I do not show my sibling enough respect.
_____   _____   My sibling does not show me enough respect.

Some specific examples of how we don't show each other enough respect include: _____

_____

_____

As you did this exercise, it's likely that one or possibly two siblings kept coming to mind. Perhaps answering these questions brought back some memories of how it was when you were kids. To fully understand the rivalry riddle, you have to go back to your family of origin and that arena in which you played out your sibling rivalries. It is there you will find the answer to the hot buttons, the feelings you can't quite explain or conquer. In the next chapter, we'll see that sibling rivalry isn't just made; it's born.

Sibling rivalry isn't just made; it's born.

Chapter 3

BATTING AT THE BOTTOM OF YOUR BIRTH ORDER

It has often occurred to me that being at the bottom of the birth order in my family has a great deal to do with my feelings of not being respected and accepted. In fact, no book on sibling relationships could be complete without at least a brief description of birth-order theory because describing one's siblings automatically brings birth order into play.

The family constellation formed by the Carlson brothers nicely outlines the three main categories of birth order, a system that was developed by psychologist Alfred Adler. Warren was the oldest or first-born. Larry was the middle child, and I was the "baby."

Although being born first has its advantages, there are built-in problems for first-borns as well. For one thing, their parents are beginners in the art of raising kids and they experiment on the first-born, usually loading on too many expectations, too much attention, and too many rules. After we became adults, my parents admitted they were harder on Warren than anyone. He got more spankings than Larry and I put together. With Warren my parents were much more demanding and much more "into" enforcing the rules. By the time I came along, they had relaxed a great deal and frankly, as the baby, I often "got away with murder."

With only adults for role models, first-borns see life as a challenge and are typically serious perfectionists who are usually reliable, conscientious, well-organized, and neat. First-borns are usually respectful of authority, eager to please, and very goal oriented.

And what happens if the first-born never has any brothers or sisters and remains an only child? You can take all of the above adjectives and characteristics and multiply them by at least ten, or, if you prefer, just add the prefix "super" to each description. Keep this only-child category in mind because later I'll explain why all three of us—Warren, Larry, and I—are, in a way, "only children."

Neat Warren and Messy Larry

Warren fits the first-born category to a T. He's always been a list maker, well-organized, reliable, and conscientious. Other good words for Warren are *meticulous* and *neat*. In fact, when Warren was in high school and Larry was in junior high, they were not always happy roommates because Larry was going through a messy stage typical of early teenagers. Today Larry is as fastidious and neat as Warren, possibly more so. But back then he wasn't always too careful about putting his things away.

On one occasion, Warren came home to find Larry's clothes strewn from one end of the room to the other (as usual), and big brother decided "enough was enough." When Larry got home, he found *all* of his clothes strewn all over the front yard, hanging from trees and bushes and thrown out on the lawn. Warren had opened the second-floor window of his room and jettisoned everything that belonged to his younger brother.

A basic rule of birth order is that the middle child usually tries to go the opposite way from the first-born. The theory holds that if the first-born is proficient in one thing, the second-born will try to carve out his or her niche in something else. Larry held true to form. While Warren became an electronics whiz, Larry became very skilled in music. Today he can play anything with a keyboard and several wind instruments as well.

Other characteristics of middle children are that they are mediators, avoiders of conflict—and independent. Larry particularly fits the "independent" slot. He hates having to abide by schedules or having his time controlled by others in any way. In short, he doesn't like to be pinned down or boxed in, which helps explain why he didn't respond when I invited him to my board meeting that week he was visiting Arizona.

In fact, Larry is so averse to being scheduled that he has never liked flying all that well because it means having to be at an airport at a given time to catch the plane! He's much better about flying now than he used to be, but in the past on annual or semiannual trips to Arizona on business, Larry would often choose to drive the eighteen hundred miles because then he could call his own shots on where he had to be and when.

How It Feels to Be "Squeezed"

Another typical feeling shared by many middle children is that they are "squeezed" between the older and the younger ones in the family. Sometimes they feel like outsiders, as if they don't belong anywhere. That's why the middle child will often be the first to go outside the home to find friends. It's this strong need for friends that helps the middle child become a good negotiator and mediator. Larry fits these categories beautifully. As president of Youth Haven Ranch, some of his strongest skills lie in management and direction of the staff.

As far as being squeezed is concerned, Larry could tell you a lot of stories about not having his own room and having to bunk either with Warren or with me, his little twerp of a brother. Larry would move back and forth between our rooms, depending on the emotional climate of the moment. Needless to say, the day Warren tossed everything Larry owned out the window, Larry moved back in with his baby brother, where messiness was seldom an issue. To begin with, I was too young to care much, and even if I had cared, Larry probably wouldn't have paid much attention.

To put things in perspective, realize that when I was born, Warren was eleven and Larry was almost six. By the time I was big enough to get a fix on what was going on, Warren seemed almost like an uncle, and Larry was my much-bigger brother whom I admired as well as feared a great deal. When we were kids, Larry and Warren were so much bigger and stronger that I never dreamed of competing with them head-to-head. I identify with the words of one later-born sibling who put it this way when talking about older brothers: "You're afraid to compete because they'll kill you."[1]

When I was a small child, Larry could make me cry just by making faces at me. I'd start wailing and Mom would come in to take my side and protect me from my "big bad brother." Of course a lot of this wailing was manipulative, which is a common characteristic of babies of the family who love to set up their older siblings to get in trouble with Mom or Dad.

Last-borns are also typically charming little show-offs; they are often the clowns who keep the family in stitches. My own last-born son, D.J., fits that category far better than I ever did. But I did acquire other baby characteristics, such as being a "people person," which undoubtedly is a reason why I went into counseling.

WHY ALL OF US WERE "ONLY CHILDREN"

Although Warren, Larry, and I follow the typical roles of first-born, middle child, and baby fairly well, there is one important variable that makes each of us, in a sense, an only child. That variable is the wide gap between each of our births. For example, when Warren was fourteen, our age-spacing order would have looked like this:

Carlson Family Siblings
Warren — 14
Larry — 8
Randy — 3

When you have a gap of five or more years between children, the entire birth-order constellation usually starts over again.

Birth-order theorists say that when you have a gap of five years or more between children, the entire birth-order constellation usually starts over again in many ways. This is not to say that the primary birth-order categories are totally void, but when Larry followed Warren by six years, that created a variable that in many ways caused Larry to have some first-born characteristics similar to Warren's.

For example, Larry turned out to be very detail-oriented and perfectionistic, and like most perfectionists he was hardest on himself. Creative and industrious, Larry became something of a legend in our family (at least to me), when he painted our entire two-story house *by himself* at age fourteen. In high school he also became a real craftsman with wood, and one of his many projects around the Carlson house included a beautiful picket fence that he built entirely on his own.

With my parents and two much older brothers for role models, I also came out with many first-born traits. Like Larry and Warren, I'm a perfectionist, although they both put me to shame with being painstaking about details. I also became reliable, conscientious, well-organized, and serious—perhaps too serious. Becoming partners with Kevin Leman, the "clown prince of 'Parent Talk,' " has done a lot to get me to "lighten up." Kevin, by the way, is also the baby of his family.

But mixed in with all those serious traits were some of the typical characteristics of the baby. Like most babies, I particularly loved celebrating birthdays and Christmas because that's when we got presents. I also became adept at trying to get other people to do things for me because I was "too little." But, paradoxically, I also grew up wanting to show those bigger brothers of mine that "I could do it too." I continually wanted to prove to them that I could be trusted and be the kind of kid they wanted their little brother to be. I didn't want them to have to worry because I was youngest or "littlest."

ONE BRIEF SHINING MOMENT OF GLORY

One of the greatest triumphs of my childhood came on the day when my brothers got me into an arm-wrestling contest with the neighborhood nerd, who was twelve years old. I was only seven, but my desperate need for my brothers' acceptance and respect pumped extra adrenaline into my veins, and somehow I beat the other kid, who admittedly wasn't all that coordinated or even that strong, even at the age of twelve. I could tell my brothers were impressed, and for at least one brief moment I basked in the glory of their respect.

My arm-wrestling victory was, however, the only highlight of my athletic career. When I tried out for Little League baseball, the coach put me on first base to see if I could stop a hot grounder. He whacked one at me, and I stopped it all right—with my teeth. That proved to be the bloody ending of my venture into baseball, and it took me a few years to work up courage to give sports another try.

Eventually, in my junior year of high school, I went out for football and spent one year on the junior varsity as third-string linebacker. We played our J.V. games on Thursday nights, and my only claim to fame was dislocating my shoulder twice. My brothers, by the way, were too busy with their own lives to make any of my games. Warren was married by then and living two hundred miles away while Larry was going to college and was seldom home during the middle of the week when I played.

Actually, I had more success on the football field by playing in the band at half-time for varsity games on Friday nights. I was no "natural musician," but I'd gotten started by taking piano lessons as early as age five. I'd always enjoyed watching Larry play, and I admired how well he could do on the piano. So when Mom wanted me to try piano, too, I started out enthusiastically, but I soon became discouraged.

I'd go to my teacher's house for lessons and then come home with my little *Thompson First Grade Piano Book* to practice. As I sat down at our piano, I'd have to push Larry's music out of the way—masterpiece compositions that looked impossible for a beginner like me. I always felt, *I'll never get there. I'll never be as good as Larry is.*

After a year and a half of piano, I quit and took saxophone instead. The sax was my dad's instrument—he used to be the leader and saxophonist in his own dance band before becoming a Christian—and I did learn to play the sax well enough to get into the high school band.

Later on I was part of what was known as the "Carlson Trio." My dad, Larry, and myself would go out to play at church functions such as father-son banquets. Dad and I were on the sax and Larry played the piano. The Carlson Trio operated for several years while I was in my late teens and early twenties. Those were great times because finally Larry and I had something in common, and I was part of a team along with him.

"RANDY FOLLOWING LARRY; DO YOU READ ME?"

It seems I was always trying to follow in my big brothers' footsteps, and this was particularly true regarding ham radio. I've already shared my memories of feeling left out as my brothers talked to exotic places far away and even used their ham radio skills to assist tornado spotters. The more I watched their ham radio exploits the more I wanted to be part of it, but neither Larry nor Warren ever had time to help me. A neighbor boy a couple of years older than I finally got me started.

My friend Jim let me use his set and taught me Morse code. When I was about to turn twelve, I passed all the tests to become a ham radio operator, novice class. I'll never forget the thrill when I put my license in a frame and tacked it up on the wall of my room so all the world could know that Randy Carlson's ham radio call letters were W-N-8-N-K-J.

My folks were proud of me, but I don't remember Warren or Larry saying much at all. Dad gave me the money to buy my own equipment, a thirty-dollar transmitter and a sixty-dollar receiver. Jim helped me hook it all up to an antenna out back. After adding the final touch (a Morse code key), I was in business. I'd sit there at night, sending Morse code messages to Jim. In fact, I sent Morse code to other hams *everywhere* because

Morse code was all a novice could send or receive at that time according to F.C.C. regulations.

The Highest Rating of All

Today there are four levels for ham radio operators: novice, general, advanced, and extra class. When I got my license, F.C.C. rules said I had to advance to the next level in one year or lose my novice license. As a typical twelve-year-old might do, I went hot and heavy on ham radio for a few months, then lost interest. At the end of the year, I lost my novice rating as well as my original call letters.

I didn't get back into ham radio until my late teens and early twenties. Then I regained my novice license and advanced in the ratings very quickly. Eventually I surpassed Larry, who never got higher than general class, and even Warren, who had achieved advanced status. Today I'm an extra-class ham radio operator and although I haven't done any ham radio in years, I could go back on the air tonight if I wished.

Why did I achieve the highest rating in ham radio? Could it be that the chubby little baby of the family set out to show his brothers he could do it? In fact, maybe he wanted to show them he could do it better than they could!

Alas! All my ham radio efforts didn't really gain me much respect and acceptance from Larry or Warren. I doubt that they were even impressed by the fact that I got to extra class while they didn't go as far. Ham radio was just a hobby with them, as it was with me, and if their baby brother wanted to work a little harder at it, who cared?

The Beginning of Sibling Rivalry

I have shared a few birth-order insights on the Carlson brothers to give you an example of how siblings may or may not connect while they're growing up together under the same roof. Obviously, there are countless birth-order combinations that can affect any sibling mix: I've already mentioned one major variable: the spacing of our three births was so wide—six years between Larry and Warren and five years between Larry and me —that, in a sense, we were three "only children." But there are many other variables that can affect every family's constellation, or, as my partner, Kevin Leman, likes to say, every "family zoo."

Suppose, for example, that Larry and I had been girls and our age spacing had looked something like this:

Warren — 14
Female — 12
Female — 8

In this kind of family, Larry could have become "Loretta," and she and Warren probably would have been serious rivals because both would have been "first-borns"—Warren, the first-born male, and Loretta, the first-born female, just two years younger. I could have become "Lucinda," and, trailing along four years behind Loretta as the "baby princess" of the family, I wouldn't have been big enough to give Loretta much competition. We probably would have grown up with a minimum of rivalry. Later on as adults, we would likely have been very close as sisters.

The most intense feelings between siblings are shared by sisters.

In *Mixed Feelings*, author Francine Klagsbrun reports that she found the most intense feelings between siblings are shared by sisters. In surveying hundreds of adult siblings, Klagsbrun used a questionnaire that measured the issue of closeness in nearly a dozen ways, and in almost every case "women reported themselves closer to their sisters in significantly greater numbers than did men to their brothers or did brothers and sisters to one another."[2]

How Birth Order Might Affect a Big Family

To give you one more example of how birth order can cause certain sibling rivalries, let's look at the family of Jessica, who had two older sisters, then two younger brothers, and finally, a baby sister. When Jessica was eleven, her family's age-spacing list would have looked something like this:

Marilyn — 15
Diane — 13
Jessica — 11

Bill — 9
Dick — 5
Marcy — 1

When I interviewed Jessica about the rivalries she feels with some of her siblings today, she was in her early fifties and planning an ambitious reconciliation program to "break the ice" that had formed over the years, particularly with her younger brother Bill.

When Jessica asked me what I thought her birth order was, I didn't tell her she was a middle child. On the contrary, she was the "baby" in a "first family" that was comprised of three girls. When her brother, Bill, came along three years later, he was the first-born *boy*, and that propitious event really started a second birth order in the family.

It was no surprise that there was rivalry between Bill and Jessica, the girl immediately above him in the family, and it appeared that the rivalry was still going on. Bill was her chief target for reconciliation because the two of them hadn't spoken for more than twenty-five years. It seems that some kind of rift started not long after Jessica married when Bill was set to graduate from high school. For some reason, long since forgotten by Jessica, Bill became upset with her and her husband on the night he graduated and wouldn't talk to them anymore.

Just last year Jessica's older sister, Marilyn, finally mentioned that she had seen Bill, and he was wondering why Jessica was still not speaking to him after all those years. That started Jessica thinking about trying to reconcile, but the old hurts were proving hard to overcome.

This was not the only rivalry in Jessica's family.

"Marilyn is really good at being the first-born leader of our family," she observed. "She has always been there to give the rest of us advice and has tried to keep people in touch with one another."

"Have all the other siblings appreciated Marilyn's leadership?" I asked.

"Everyone but Diane. Because she's just two years younger than Marilyn, she's always tried to compete with her and never wanted to listen to her advice very much. It was as if Marilyn were always trying to become top dog. She always acted as if she were a little too good for the rest of us."

This is often the way younger siblings, as adults, perceive their first-born brother or sister. Meanwhile, the first-born is driven by a sense of responsibility and leadership that makes him or her feel this role is a duty, not an option. In return for the effort he or she expends in carrying out this leadership role, the first-born expects younger siblings to defer to his or her judgment.

Because Diane refused to play the role of protégé to Marilyn as they were growing up, there was some rivalry and tension, but according to Jessica, they were able to resolve that when they reached adulthood. As I continued interviewing Jessica, it became apparent that most of the rivalry feelings were between the three older children who formed one part of the family and the three younger siblings who formed the other.

According to Jessica, her younger brother Bill, from whom she had been estranged for so long, was her dad's favorite—until Dick came along five years later.

"Dick got away with murder," Jessica recalled. "He smashed up two cars but somehow Dad managed to replace them pretty much out of his own pocket. All of us older girls had to work really hard for our cars."

And what of Marcy, the last-born baby princess of the family? It turned out she was even more favored than Dick. As Jessica put it, "Marcy got to go to college while the rest of us didn't."

What Jessica described concerning Dick and Marcy, the two youngest children in the family, is another common variable of birth order. As parents grow older and have more children, they usually relax the rules. Not only do they tend to baby the youngest children, but they often have more money to spend on them. In other words, the parents who parented Dick and Marcy were different from those who parented Marilyn, Diane, and Jessica. Because the older children perceived that the younger children were favored, it caused a rivalry among all of them that still exists today to some extent. While Jessica's major problem was with her younger brother Bill, she admitted that she had seldom gotten together with Dick or Marcy over the years, and she was hoping she could remedy that situation too.

Another typical birth-order variable that can cause rivalry among siblings happens when one child becomes "exceptional" for some reason. Perhaps the child has a serious illness or accident and is crippled or handicapped in some way. This means that child will get a lot more attention from the parents, who will remind the other siblings, "Don't be so hard on Billy. You should always help your brother."

When the birth order is skewed in this fashion, the scarcity mentality works overtime. While the other siblings continually feel somewhat guilty for resenting Billy at least a little bit, they're still thinking, *I always get less—Billy is more important.*

To pinpoint where certain frictions with your own siblings could have begun when you were children, fill in the following age-spacing list:

First-born (name) _____ Present age _____

Second-born (name) _____ Present age _____

Third-born (name) _____ Present age _____

Fourth-born (name) _____ Present age _____

(Add more lines as needed)

Use the following questions to analyze how your family constellation has possibly affected your sibling relationships, especially today as adults.

1. Did the first-born in the family have to compete with an aggressive second-born who wanted to take over the "top spot"? __Yes __No If yes, in what way did this happen?_____
   _____
   _____

2. Was the baby of the family the "spoiled brat who got away with murder"? __Yes __No If so, how did the other siblings relate to the baby?_____

_____

_____

3. Did you or any of your siblings receive extra attention or special privileges of any kind due to illness, injury, or for some other reason? ___Yes ___No If so, how did this affect your relationships to your siblings then—and now?_____

_____

_____

4. If you were the first-born in your family, how has your birth order affected your sibling relationships overall? Positively ___ Negatively ___
Describe: _____

_____

_____

5. If you are a middle child, how has your birth order affected your sibling relationships? Have you ever felt squeezed? ___Yes ___No When and how did this occur? _____

_____

_____

6. If you are the baby of your family, how has your birth order affected your sibling relationships? _____

_____

_____

7. If you were the baby and you were spoiled by your parents, were your older siblings jealous? ___Yes ___No Did your older siblings discount or disrespect you because you were the "little twerp"? ___Yes ___No How do your siblings treat you today? _

_____

_____

YOUR BRANCH OF THE FAMILY TREE

I've given you only a taste of how the family constellation brings certain pressures to bear and causes certain siblings to compete more than others. But whatever birth-order limb of the family tree you land on, you still become a unique personality with your own way of looking at life and at your siblings. Who you become after you land on that particular limb depends on a lot of things. Adlerian counselors believe that during the first few years of life, we all develop a life goal and a lifestyle as we cope with growing up and discover what works or doesn't work for us.

As we explore the rivalry riddle further, we need to take a look at how this lifestyle forms. Every sibling develops a sense *The little brother or sister you once were, you still are.* of identity within the family, and as he or she carves out that sense of identity, the child learns to take on a certain role. In most cases, the role you learn to play as a child is the role you will play as an adult. The little brother or sister you once were, you still are. In the next chapter we'll look more closely at just why this is true, even after "all these years."

Chapter 4

SIBLINGS: PLAYERS ON THE FAMILY'S STAGE

While birth order creates our specific limb of the family tree, it remains for each of us, from the moment we are born, to cope with life, experimenting to see what works and what doesn't. In so doing, we set certain basic goals. If we reach them, fine; if we don't, we abandon them and try new goals.

Out of all this we develop a plan to make sense out of life. In the Adlerian school of counseling, this life plan is also called a "style of life," or lifestyle. When Alfred Adler, the pioneer in the field of individual psychology, coined the term *lifestyle*, he wasn't thinking at all about how we dress, the kind of car we drive, or the type of home we live in. Adler was far more interested in how we live *inside* the body God gave us and how we operate daily. Each of us has a unique personal lifestyle, and out of this we develop what people recognize as our "personality."

The paint on your personality portrait dries early, and by age six or seven your personal lifestyle is pretty well set. Then the rest of your growing-up years are spent touching up your portrait as you learn to play a certain role in life.

The paint on your personality portrait dries early . . . by age six or seven your personal lifestyle is pretty well set.

When I talk about "playing a role," I'm not using the term in the sense of being phony or hypocritical. Exactly the opposite is true. As you take on your role, you are definitely being you, which has its positive and negative aspects. In other words, you have your strengths and your weaknesses just as your siblings do, and all of you perfect your roles as you grow up on the family stage. As you go on into adult life, you keep the role you learned as a child. You may put the basic portrait in a very nice frame, and you may touch up the portrait a bit or perhaps hang it in a favorable light to impress your friends. But when it's all said and done, the adult sibling you are today is in large part the sibling you became as a child.

FALLING INTO ROLE CATEGORIES

In one sense, everyone develops a role that is unique to him or her, but for practical purposes, we need to look at several broad role categories most people fall into. And, of course, it's not unusual for a person to have traits represented by more than one role. Each of us is a complex blend as a result of genetics, birth order, and family atmosphere (the effect our parents and siblings have had upon us). Your parents had a great deal to do with the lifestyle you developed, but as you interacted with your siblings, they also helped you develop that lifestyle and the role you decided to play. As Jane Greer observes:

> Roles serve many purposes, not least organizing what might otherwise be domestic chaos. Roles contribute a sense of order to the family. They provide a means for people to know where they belong in family activities. Their role is also the part you play in the family. In this sense, the family is a stage and your role is part of a drama.

By complex and often unconscious processes, family members cast one another in different roles.[1]

Following is a list of sixteen typical roles that you may see played out among the siblings in any family:

1. *The confident, controlling one.* Typically, this is the family's first-born, who may try to parent his or her younger siblings.

2. *The responsible, dependable one.* Again, this is usually the task of the first-born, but it's a role that a child of any birth-order might take. My brothers and I were all "only children" by virtue of being born so far apart, but perhaps the most responsible one in the family was Larry, the middle son, and he still sees himself that way today.

3. *The brainy one.* This child is the family scholar—anything less than an A is a disaster.

4. *The charming, witty one.* Usually this one is the most well-liked child in the family.

5. *The social one.* Often called the "social butterfly," this child has many friends and is popular outside of the family.

6. *The isolated one.* Usually, this child is a self-centered loner and has great abilities to be on his or her own.

7. *The sick one.* The family hypochondriac is ill or claims to be ill far more often than anyone else.

8. *The rebellious one.* This child can wind up as the irresponsible "black sheep" who often brings shame or disgrace to the family.

9. *The manipulative one.* Typically, this is the last-born child. He or she may be a spoiled brat who gets the rest of the family to comply with his or her wishes.

10. *The goody-goody one.* This child has a "higher moral code" than the rest of the family. An offshoot of the goody-goody is the person who always has to be right

and lives in mortal fear of making an error. Being right is literally an obsession.

11. *The driving, ambitious one.* This is the ultimate competitor who is constantly trying to reach a goal. Winning is crucial, if not everything.

12. *The compliant, pleasing one.* With a strong need to be liked, this child will try to please everyone possible. He or she is very sensitive to criticism and is crushed when not given total and instant approval. Often this child becomes the family C.E.O (chief emotional officer).

13. *The persecuted one.* This child often appears in one of two subcategories—victim or martyr. Victims are "accident prone." They often engage in self-pity or seek the sympathy or pity of others. Martyrs are a bit different since they put more emphasis on "suffering for a noble cause." They are good at showing moral indignation, or sometimes they suffer in silence at the hands of those who take advantage of them.

14. *The inferior one.* Characterized as not being able to do anything right, this child is often awkward or clumsy to boot. He or she will take few risks and will try to do only the easiest things, where success is a sure thing. Sometimes called "a walking inferiority complex."

15. *The shy, quiet one.* This child stays in the background and doesn't appreciate being given attention or having to be "up front."

16. *The logical, rational one.* With an intellectual approach to life, this child takes pride in being logical and thinking things through. He or she keeps feelings well subdued and doesn't like displays of emotion. Often "talks a good game."

Many other lifestyles, or roles, could be listed. As a rule, two siblings will seldom take the same role in a family. Don't expect your siblings to be like you. Each child of you will develop your own unique view of life and a special way of interacting with others.

MARY LOU'S ROLE

For an example of how people live out their life roles, let's go back to Mary Lou, the woman who was described in chapter 2. As the baby sister of the family of four boys and one girl, she could have easily become the "baby princess," spoiled, helpless, and manipulative. Instead, she "got no respect" from her four big brothers, she said. Mary Lou became a compliant child who felt it was her duty to keep others happy. Her role turned out to be a blend of the compliant, pleasing child and the responsible, dependable one. And when her mother suffered a stroke in her later years, Mary Lou became the chief emotional officer of the family. Or perhaps she had already assumed that role, and caring for her mother because her four brothers lived in other states only solidified it.

As Mary Lou described her brothers, it was apparent that their roles included everything from controlling manipulator to irresponsible rebel. Only one of them had followed through with his agreement to help with his ailing mother's support, and most of them did not bother to contact her in any way, not even with a card or gift at Christmas.

As I talked with Mary Lou, at first I feared that a part of her life role would include being victim or even martyr. But I didn't hear a lot of self-pity in what she was telling me, and when she obviously was willing to stand up to her brothers, I realized she was not a victim. When she confronted her brothers with her "wake-up-and-smell-the-coffee" letter, there was tension for a while, but eventually they did take a more active role in helping with their ailing mother.

BIG BROTHERS

One of the more interesting "Parent Talk" programs we have done on adult sibling relationships featured an on-the-air reunion between Jeff, a first-born brother, and Carol, his younger sister. They seldom saw each other although they lived in the same community. Carol and Jeff hadn't talked on the phone, written, or even exchanged birthday or Christmas cards for years. The only time they got together was at infrequent family functions, so we felt fortunate when Jeff, in particular, agreed to come on the show by phone.

As the reunion progressed, it became clear that these two siblings had played far different roles in their families. Jeff saw Carol as a combination of confident and controlling along with being manipulative. As he put it, "She usually got her way—well, much of her own way—with our parents." He even admitted that he wished he could have been as verbal and controlling as his sister was, but his quiet personality kept him from even trying.

"We can get along OK if we're in a group where she's very outgoing and friendly and fun to be around," Jeff explained, "but once we get alone and talking, we don't hit it off very well at all. She seems to try to take control. She wants to know who I'm dating, why I'm not married, and what my plans are. She sounds like a reporter doing a report for the six o'clock news."

It wasn't too hard to recognize that Jeff's life role was a combination of the isolated loner and the shy and quiet child who really didn't appreciate a lot of attention or having his business known by other people, not even his sister. Carol admitted she is very inquisitive and that she does interrogate her brother whenever she sees him—because that's simply her nature. She's curious about what he is doing. But Jeff saw it as more than curiosity—as literally interfering in his life.

When we asked Jeff what he would do if he could wave a magic wand and change his sister in any way, he answered, "I would basically have her try not to control every situation, just enjoy it for what it is."

But from her perspective, Carol also had expectations—and disappointments. As the younger sibling, she'd always expected her older brother, first-born of the family, to be strong and assertive, someone she could trust and look up to. Jeff had never really fulfilled that role, and Carol admitted that when they got together she often ended up asking him questions in a tone that said, *When are you going to be the big brother that I want you to be?*

One of the most poignant moments of their on-the-air reunion came during this exchange:

CAROL: You know, Jeff, I don't know if you remember, but when I was a really little girl, in first or second grade, I wrote you a note and it said, "Dear Jeff, Do you love me?" I never got a response, but one day I was down in the laundry room with Mommy and we were going through all the laundry and we found that note in your pants pocket. At the bottom, you had put in big letters, "No." Do you remember that?

JEFF: No, I don't.

CAROL: Well, I have never forgotten that, and it really hurt me. I think maybe sometime way back I decided, "I'm not going to be close to my brother, Jeff." I really regret that now.

As their on-the-air exchange was ending, I asked Jeff, "If you could get one thing out of your relationship with Carol, what would it be?"

"I guess one thing I'd like to be able to do is just sit down and be friends," Jeff responded. "Now every time we sit down it's like an interrogation."

And then I asked Carol, "If you could ask for one thing out of your relationship with Jeff, what would it be?"

Carol responded, "I realize that I bug him with my constant questions and wanting him to be someone he really isn't. I'm praying for the strength to change my expectations. I hope that someday I can accept him where he is right now and realize what he has to offer as a part of my family. I know he has unique gifts and talents that I have never even discovered."

Since their on-the-air reunion, I've done some follow-up on Jeff and Carol and am happy to report that there has been some real progress in their relationship. They have gotten together once or twice for an evening of food and relaxation, and Carol assures me she didn't play her usual role of critical interrogator quite as much. There is real hope for Jeff and Carol, and much of the credit lies with the younger sister who not only recognized she was a big part of her sibling rivalry problem, but was willing to change to make things better. (For more on developing a strategy for reaching out to an estranged sibling, see Chapters 7 and 8.)

THE CARLSON BROTHERS' ROLES

As I analyze the roles played by my brothers and me, I see myself as a curious combination of compliant-pleaser/victim mixed with the role of the competent and dependable one. It isn't too hard to trace where I learned to play the competent, dependable role. With my parents and much older brothers for role models, I developed these only-child traits plus a lot more, such as being conscientious, perfectionistic, and serious.

My serious side gives a hint about how I came out a pleaser/victim. Most of my early childhood memories center around one word: *disaster*. Dislocating my shoulder twice while playing high school football and taking a ground ball in the teeth during Little League tryouts were traumatic incidents, but my disasters go back a lot further than that. At age six or seven I remember riding my bide in a field near our home when some kid hollered at me, and as I looked back I veered off the path right into a tree and went flying.

Another early memory I have concerns a tornado that went right over Muskegon, Michigan, where we lived when I was around five years old. Our whole family had to take refuge in the fruit cellar. Fortunately, the tornado never dropped its funnel, but it sounded as if a freight train had gone right through our house, and I was scared to death.

In *Unlocking the Secrets of Your Childhood Memories*, I point out that whenever you analyze an early childhood memory, it's important to attach a feeling to the clearest part of that memory.[2] The feeling I attach to my memory of the tornado is stark fear. I was certain we were all going to die. When I think of the other childhood memories I've mentioned, I also associate feelings of pain, humiliation, and embarrassment.

One of my main problems was getting my brothers to pay attention to me, and I can recall the time I pestered them a little too much, especially Warren. I was a chubby little five year old when I walked into Warren's room one day, uninvited, while he and Larry were fiddling with Warren's ham radio. At sixteen, Warren didn't appreciate little brothers hanging around, and I think he was in an extra-bad mood that morning to boot. He told me I had three seconds to make tracks or he would plug me with his BB gun. I turned to go but I took my time because I thought he really didn't mean it. Big mistake! When I didn't move fast enough for him, he grabbed his BB gun from behind the door and snapped off a shot that nailed me in my ample little behind as I tried to run.

Getting bushwhacked by my big brother was humiliating and painful, but I can't remember any other incidents of a similar nature. As a rule, Warren and Larry would content themselves with teasing their baby brother, whom they fondly referred to as "Fat Butt." I have another early memory of a time when our family was planning to go camping and stay in a cabin on the shores of Lake Michigan. When Warren learned I'd be sleeping in one of the rooms all alone, he got a big kick out of telling me the spiders would be there to "bite you right on your chubby little butt." I ran crying to my mother and told her what Warren had said. Much to my satisfaction, he had to sleep in that room instead of me!

When I add up all these childhood memories, I always come out with the same emotions: embarrassment, a little bit of hurt (sometimes more than a little bit!), and fear. It seems that as I worked out my own personality portrait, I found life to be a very challenging place where I was apt to run into trouble more often than not. I think all this helped steer me in the direction of playing the victim. Later I also became very much a pleaser, an uncommon characteristic for a male. But being a pleaser seemed to work for me because it kept the world off my back. Over all, my motto turned out to be: "Be careful . . . don't take many risks, and don't make waves—try to keep everybody happy."

Although he was a middle child, Larry, five years my senior and six years behind Warren, had enough only-child traits to develop the role of "responsible one." To this day, he still drops by my parents' permanent home in Michigan to be sure the house is in good repair. During a recent conversation, he told me, "I always felt responsible. That's why I painted our house when I was only fourteen and built that picket fence. I've always seen my role as 'the guy who keeps things fixed around here.' "

But in addition to being responsible, Larry also plays the role of the rational, logical, "detail person." He clearly recalls feeling very irritated when the tornado went through our town and hail the size of golf balls fell. Why did he feel irritated? Because the hail broke eleven windows in our house—not nine or ten, but exactly eleven!

Despite Warren's occasional fits of impatience with his little brothers (tossing Larry's clothes out the window and nailing me with the BB gun), he really turned out to be a responsible perfectionist blended with a bit of the compliant pleaser. His need to do well and be liked by his friends and associates drove him at a pace that caused him to burn out in his corporate field of endeavor. At present, he is recovering his health after several years of medical disability.

WHAT ROLES DO YOU AND YOUR SIBLING PLAY?

Now that you've gotten a taste of how to recognize roles, use the previous list of sixteen roles to see if you can identify your and your siblings' roles. Keep in mind that these categories are not hard-and-fast descriptions but only broad classifications to help you identify the various parts you and your siblings have played and are probably still playing on the family stage:

Identifying Sibling Roles

Role(s) I play: _____
Comments: _____

Role(s) sibling I (name) _____ plays: _____
Comments: _____

Role(s) sibling 2 (name) _____ plays: _____
Comments: _____

(If you have more than two siblings, use the margins or write on a small piece of paper that can be clipped to this page.)

If you are having a little trouble pinning down a certain sibling's role, you may find it beneficial to use the following "lifestyle assessment." Listed on the left are twenty-seven characteristics, and on the right are spaces for listing the siblings who are the most and least like that particular characteristic. Write the names of those siblings in the proper spaces and include yourself where appropriate. If you see that you're not listing yourself, simply circle the rating you would be closest to—most or least.

Lifestyle Assessment

1. Hardest worker	Most_____	Least_____
2. Lackadaisical	Most_____	Least_____
3. Sense of humor	Most_____	Least_____
4. Critical of others	Most_____	Least_____
5. Conforming	Most_____	Least_____
6. Lazy	Most_____	Least_____
7. Bossy	Most_____	Least_____
8. Courageous	Most_____	Least_____
9. Fearful	Most_____	Least_____
10. Materialistic	Most_____	Least_____
11. Idealistic	Most_____	Least_____
12. Sensitive	Most_____	Least_____
13. Charming	Most_____	Least_____
14. Crabby	Most_____	Least_____
15. Cheerful	Most_____	Least_____
16. Strong	Most_____	Least_____
17. Complainer	Most_____	Least_____
18. Weak	Most_____	Least_____
19. Kind	Most_____	Least_____
20. Spoiled	Most_____	Least_____
21. Selfish	Most_____	Least_____
22. Best grades in school	Most_____	Least_____
23. Worst grades in school	Most_____	Least_____
24. Has faith in others	Most_____	Least_____
25. Has faith in God	Most_____	Least_____

26. Liked by father	Most_____ Least_____
27. Liked by mother	Most_____ Least_____

After finishing the above lifestyle assessment, look for any recurring names. Are you at one extreme or other? Are you neither the most or least of anything? Going over these characteristics will tell you how you perceive yourself and your siblings in some key areas. It can also explain why certain siblings took on certain roles.

As you will note in the list of characteristics, there are both positive and negative traits. These traits have guided you into playing a certain role that may be healthy or unhealthy. As Jane Greer points out, "Sometimes we go along with a role because it provides a sense of where we fit into the family, sometimes because the forces defining us are too powerful to resist, sometimes we find the role itself flattering and positive, and sometimes we don't know how to manage the anger we feel about our role. Sometimes we even go along out of spite: 'If that's what they think I am, then that's what I'll be!' "[3]

Greer goes on to point out that we get lots of advice not only from parents and siblings, but from friends, other relatives, and teachers on what role we must play. Ultimately, however, we have to sort all this out and decide where we fit in our own personal drama. Each person has to decide what it means to be a good child, a good sibling, a good spouse, a good parent.

As we juggle our various roles and the expectations that go along with them, we build a sense of identity; but, ironically enough, in so doing we may limit how much of our real personalities we express because we're trying to meet the different roles we are expected to assume. "This is why," writes Greer, "we may end up feeling that there isn't a good 'fit' between who we are and the roles we have taken on."[4]

Perhaps you feel you played a role all your life that doesn't fit who you really are. If it's an unhealthy role, such as the rebellious black sheep or the persecuted victim, there is still time to make new choices. One of the best ways to determine if you still identify with an unhealthy role is to focus on how you interact with your adult siblings today.

WHEN YOU GO HOME

I talk with some clients and callers to "Parent Talk" who claim they have shed the role they played as a child and they're really "different people" now. I tell them I understand how they feel, but as a rule the role we learned as a child is still there under any slick or polished veneer we may have put over it.

Often when you "go home" again, to a family reunion for example, you are likely to experience one of those sibling moments that will bring out your original role. For example, remember Peggy and her five siblings who all had to go home to be with their mom as she died? As their mother lay there getting weaker it was a sibling moment, indeed, and the pressure finally erupted into a fistfight between two brothers who had often gotten into such battles as kids.

Unpleasant sibling moments don't always involve total explosions or all-out violence. They can happen in all kinds of settings, and usually the "law of sameness" operates. This law says:

**The more things change,
the more they stay the same.**

The years go by. Siblings may grow up, get married, have children of their own, buy homes, sell homes, get different jobs, and go through all of the many changes that happen in all of our lives. Nonetheless, those roles we learned as children are still the same, and what used to happen then will happen years later in one form or another.

When I interviewed Rachel for this book, she told me she is one of ten children, born eighth in the family. She has three sisters and six brothers. Most of her brothers are quite a bit older than she is, and there lies the problem. As we talked, she mentioned how much fun it was to get together on an annual basis with her sisters. When I asked her why her brothers weren't included, it led to the following dialogue:

RACHEL: I don't know. We just thought it would be fun to have it "girls only." A couple of years ago we had a family reunion and eight of the ten kids managed to get there for that. Because I was born eighth, I was always treated as the little kid while we were all growing up. My older brothers, in particular, really followed the pecking order. They were always lording it over me and letting me know they had more power than I did—stuff like that.

At that reunion, even though I was thirty-one years old, they still treated me like I was a lot younger than they were. As soon as we all walked into my parents' home, my older brothers assumed their ordinal positions and all the "rights" they thought went along with that. It was obvious they didn't regard me as an adult, and they treated me as if I were still six or seven or maybe ten years old. The funny thing is, I started going along with it! Later, my husband, who came with me to the reunion, pointed this out and I was shocked when I realized he was right. Since then, I've much preferred to get together with my sisters.

RANDY: What role would you say you played in your family while you were growing up? Have you always felt a strong need to keep things running smoothly in the family—to comply, for example, with what the older ones wanted?

RACHEL: Well, as a matter of fact, that describes me pretty well. I've always been something of a pleaser, but I was fortunate enough to marry a man who has helped me be more my own person and learn to say no, for example.

RANDY: And since then you've just had get-togethers with your sisters. What does this say about your relationship to your brothers?

RACHEL: Well, obviously I've got some work to do there. Maybe I'll talk to my sisters about having another big family reunion. Then I can test just how much I have changed. I'll find out if I'll let my brothers put me in the little kid's place again.

Before ending my interview with Rachel I observed that she needs to develop a strategy for how she'll approach that next family reunion and her older brothers. I suggested she get together with her husband and work out the very phrases or comebacks she will use the next time they try to treat her like a ten-year-old. Also, it would be wise for her to confront them one-on-one and not in front of the entire family group. When you approach siblings with whom you have tensions or problems, you need to have a constructive plan that you hope will lead to a better relationship, not more tension or hostility. (For more on developing strategies for approaching your siblings, see Chapters 7 and 8.)

PRIVATE LOGIC

The most important step in analyzing the various roles or lifestyles being played by you and your siblings is to compare them to see where they complement each other or where they cause conflict. A tool that you can find useful here is "individual private logic," another important part of Alfred Adler's lifestyle theories. This theory holds that all of us work out our own private logic as we grow up. Basic to that private logic is how any individual would complete three statements:

I am _____.

Others are _____.

The world is _____.

For example, a competent controller type might say:

- "I am comfortable when I do things my way."
- "Other people are not quite as capable as I am and need my help to get things right."
- "The world is usually disorganized and chaotic, and my job is to do something about it."

Another example of individual private logic would be the compliant pleaser who might say:

- "I am unsure of my abilities, even though Mom always told me I was a good kid."

- "Other people are demanding. I always have to jump a little higher to keep them happy."
- "The world is a hard place where I'm always having to measure up."

We could develop basic private logic statements for all sixteen categories listed in this chapter, but to help you focus on your sibling relationship, let's limit our private logic observations to two key perceptions:

I am _____

My siblings are _____

Going back to the case studies mentioned earlier, here's how Mary Lou, the compliant pleaser and family C.E.O., would complete some of these statements:

- "I am a nice person who gets taken advantage of and will go to great lengths to keep things running smoothly, especially for my mother."
- "My siblings are irresponsible, flaky, and inconsiderate."

I believe Carol, the competent interrogator, would put her statements this way:

- "I am inquisitive and curious because it helps me stay on top of my world."
- "My siblings are disappointing, especially my brother Jeff, who won't be a 'take charge' kind of guy whom I can look up to."

As for Jeff, the quiet withdrawn one, I believe he might say:

- "I am a nice guy who minds his own business, and I wish others would do the same."
- "My siblings are too nosy—they bug me, especially my sister, Carol."

And what about the Carlson brothers? First-born Warren, the dependable pleaser, told me:

- "I am a nice guy who has always worked hard and had a lot of heat."
- "My siblings are people I don't know as well as I would like. I want to reconnect with them at this time in my life."

Larry, the responsible, rationalist middle child, put it this way:

- "I am not always appreciated or given credit for what I do. I'm most happy when I'm in control of the situation."
- "My siblings are all tied up with their own problems. They're not that concerned about mine."

As I considered the private logic that Warren and Larry shared with me, it helped put my own sibling problems in better perspective, particularly when I filled out these two private logic statements for myself:

- "I am more concerned with pleasing others than myself."
- "My siblings are busy with their own agendas. They're not as impressed by or interested in my achievements as I would like them to be."

Obviously, the Carlson brothers all see each other in the same way—too busy and preoccupied to show interest in one another! There's a good reason for our busyness, which I'll explain in Chapter 5 when I talk about family mottoes. But if the three of us want to connect better and have our relationships go to a deeper level, it's obvious we will all have to slow down and take more time to really know each other.

Now Try It Yourself

Now that you've seen several examples, try filling out a private logic analysis for yourself and your siblings. First, state your own private logic:

I am _____

_____

My siblings are _____

_____

Next, enter what you believe sibling number one (name: _____) would say. Try to come as close to his or her private logic as you can:

I am _____

_____

My siblings are _____

_____

Now write what you think sibling number two (name: _____) would say:

I am _____

_____

My siblings are _____

_____

Obviously, you may have had more trouble writing down your siblings' private logic than your own. That's to be expected, but don't get discouraged. Keep working at it because the better you get at deducing your siblings' private logic, the more you enable yourself to "get behind their eyes" and see how they perceive their world—particularly the part you play in it. And the more you understand your siblings' private logic, the more you will be capable of making necessary changes to improve your relationships with them. We'll be looking at that much more closely in Part 2 of this book.

MAKING CHANGES

Although your personality developed very early there is still much you can do to change or at least modify your private logic, your lifestyle, and the role you have been playing on your family stage. And if you are a Christian, your chances are even better because you have the Holy Spirit as an ally.

There is, of course, no magical path to instant change. God doesn't force us to make changes; He only provides the gracious means of forgiveness and endless chances to try again when we fail. But I know from personal experience that progress is possible. I've worked hard at breaking my own unhealthy cycle of being the compliant pleaser/victim. Through much prayer, trial and error—and an occasional kick in the pants from my wife, Donna, as well as a few trusted friends and mentors—I'm doing much better. And I'm also having success in making my life role blend better with the roles of my siblings, something we'll get into in more detail in later chapters.

Becoming a parent has also done a lot to change my pleaser attitude. I've learned that daddies can't be pleasers or overly concerned about everybody liking them. Daddies have to be leaders who love their families so much they do what is best, even if it's unpopular at the moment.

The roots of rivalry go deep. Keep in mind, however, that just because you want to change your life role doesn't mean you're going to have instant improvement in relating to your siblings. The roots of rivalry go deep, and it may take a long time before you see any noticeable effect. In the next chapter, we'll talk about where rivalry starts—*in the family atmosphere.*

What kind of parents did you have and what was their parenting style? In particular, how much comparing did they do among you and your sibs? Was there any favoritism, and how fervent was the competition among all of you? Sometimes siblings can be competing without really calling it that. I think that's very true of myself and my brothers, and in Chapter 5 I'll explain why.

Chapter 5

COMING TO GRIPS WITH THE GREEN-EYED MONSTER

Since this chapter will focus on jealousy and competition, let's start with a little quiz. Which former president of the United States made the following remark?

"I'm shadowboxing in a match the shadow is always going to win."

> a. John F. Kennedy
> b. Jimmy Carter
> c. George Bush

Playing "Second Banana"

Although he was never quoted as saying, "Mom always loved my brother Joe best," John F. Kennedy, thirty-fifth president of the United States, did know what it was like to shadow-box in a match the shadow would always win. From early on, he would often get into fistfights with his older brother, Joe Jr., and being younger, plus skinny and sickly, he'd always lose. Although their mother, Rose Kennedy, deplored the fisticuffs, she still encouraged (actually demanded) competition among her children. If you were a Kennedy, you were taught to play to win, and if you lost or got hurt you were not to cry, only try harder next time.

To say there was sibling rivalry among Jack Kennedy and his siblings would be an understatement. In particular, he was always trying to outdo Joe Jr., but he seldom won. One of his most memorable defeats came on the day they raced on bicycles, going around the block in opposite directions. As they both came down toward the finish line, head-on, neither boy gave an inch. Joe Jr. came out of the inevitable crash unscathed while Jack needed twenty-eight stitches.[1]

One of the few times Jack ever came out on top was after they had both gone into the navy during World War II. In the early years of the war, neither one had seen any action and while both of them were upset about that, Joe Jr. was even more chagrined because his younger brother had earned the rank of lieutenant junior grade, while he was still an ensign.

Finally, in 1943, with the help of a timely word from his highly influential father to the undersecretary of the navy, a personal friend, Jack was shipped out to the Pacific for PT boat duty. Meanwhile, Joe Jr. had been assigned to flying routine patrols in the Caribbean, far from any real action. Jack had finally won one, and it practically broke Joe Jr.'s heart as tales of his little brother's heroism came trickling back from the South Pacific.

Joe Jr. would spend most of two tours of duty flying patrol, including antisubmarine missions over the English Channel. But during those months, he "never saw an enemy submarine, never dropped a bomb, or fired a shot."[2] During his second tour, he did take part in the D-Day invasion of Normandy but overall he did nothing to distinguish himself despite his desperate attempts to be a hero.

With his extended tour almost over, Joe Jr. was packed to go home when he heard about the need for experienced pilots to fly a hazardous, top-secret mission. He volunteered and died in a blinding, unexplained explosion after being airborne for only twenty-eight minutes.

But Joe Jr.'s death did not do away with the rivalry between the two brothers. His memory was always there. When a final letter, written by Joe Jr. just before his last mission to explain why he had volunteered, arrived at the Kennedy home, his father put his head in his hands and said over and over that the best part of his life was finished.

It is no wonder that his younger brother, Jack, felt he was still competing with the memory of his brother's potential. After he got into politics, he would tell volunteers working in his campaign, "I'm just filling Joe's shoes. If he were alive, I'd never be in this."[3]

John F. Kennedy's biography is a graphic illustration of how competition can become a virtual way of life in a family. Many parents

Competition always carries with it a high price.

believe "healthy" competition among family members is beneficial because it encourages individual development and teaches children how to be ready for the rigors of living in the real world. (For reasons why competition in the family is harmful, see Chapter 12.) But competition always carries with it a high price, and while it motivated Jack Kennedy to reach greater heights it was a mixed blessing because of his struggles with the green-eyed monster of jealousy and the ghost of his brother, Joe Jr.

JACOB AND ESAU: UNHEALTHY COMPETITION

Although Cain and Abel go down as history's first sibling rivals, there is no question that the most flagrant biblical case of parental favoritism and destructive competition between siblings was that of Jacob and Esau, twin sons of Isaac and Rebecca. Their story, which begins in Genesis 25, says that even while still in the womb, the brothers struggled together violently, and when Esau was born first, Jacob came out holding onto his heel, as if to say, *Watch out, Big Brother, I'm right behind you.*

In classic birth-order fashion, Jacob became the skillful hunter and a man of the field while his second-born brother went another direction becoming a "mild man, dwelling in tents" (Gen. 25:27). And as many parents are prone to do, Rebecca and Isaac had their favorites between the boys. "Isaac loved Esau, because he ate of his game, but Rebecca loved Jacob" (Gen. 25:28).

Spurred on by his mother, Jacob became a classic schemer, always looking for a way to outdo his bigger, stronger, and apparently dim-witted brother who spent most of his time tramping the fields in search of game. Meanwhile, back in the tents, peaceful Jacob became something of a gourmet cook. One day, after Jacob had prepared a pot of tasty stew, Esau came in famished from hunting and when he asked for some food, Jacob said, in effect, "Sure, you can have some stew if you're willing to trade your birthright for it."

The birthright was no small item. It entitled the first-born son of the family to a double portion of his father's inheritance and a more honorable position than his brother, but even more important it guaranteed the covenant blessings God had promised to Abraham and his descendants.[4]

Esau put so little stock in his birthright that he gladly traded it away for one bowl of stew and some bread and went on his way without much thought about the whole incident. Years later, Jacob, with his mother's assistance, completed the subverting of his brother by tricking his old and almost blind father into giving him the all-important oral blessing that would make him absolutely number one in the family and the one who would become the Lord's representative in the patriarchal line.

While Esau was out hunting to get his father some game, Rebecca helped Jacob don a clever disguise that fooled Isaac into believing he was giving his blessing to his first-born son. When Esau returned and learned that his father had given his younger brother the blessing, thereby making Jacob the head of the household and sentencing Esau to be his servant, Esau asked his father if there was a blessing for him and was told there was none.

Murderous jealousy and a desire for revenge filled Esau's heart, and he planned to kill his brother just as soon as his father had died. Rebecca learned about Esau's plot, however, and warned her son to flee for his life. There followed many years of estrangement between the two brothers.

Today comparatively few parents formally bless their offspring in a biblical sense,[5] but all children still need their parents' blessing in the form of unconditional love and acceptance. When one sib feels he or she was not accepted and loved by his or her parents as much as another sib, it can cause serious rivalry—what is often referred to as "unresolved issues" or "differences of opinion."

> *All children still need their parents' blessing in the form of unconditional love and acceptance.*

Whatever siblings choose to call the tension between themselves, it can keep them at odds or perhaps at other ends of the country, never communicating for year after year. "Mom (and/or Dad) always loved you best," is a lot more than a funny line in a Smothers Brothers comedy routine. For thousands of siblings, it is a plaintive cry of frustration or even anger and rage.

PROGRAMMED FOR RIVALRY

If you have unresolved issues or open rivalry with another sibling today, it could be that one or both of you is a victim of parental programming that has put you at odds. Perhaps your parents openly played favorites, or maybe they just encouraged competition. In my surveys for this book, 55 percent reported there was a favorite sibling, but respondents were split fifty-fifty on whether they were the favorite or a sibling was.

Was there competition or favoritism within your family? Take the following quiz and check the statements that apply to you. The more checks you have, the more competition or favoritism was present as you were growing up.

Assessing Competition or Favoritism in Your Family

_____ 1. I often felt that my parent(s) compared me in favorable or unfavorable ways with one or more of my siblings.

_____ 2. My parent(s) would make unfavorable comments about their own siblings (my aunts or uncles).

_____ 3. What I accomplished seemed more important to my parents than who I was as a person.

_____ 4. I was put in direct competition (in sports, music, academics, etc.) with my siblings.

_____ 5. In my family, there was a "favorite" child who was recognized as such on a spoken (or unspoken) basis.

Sometimes parents make no attempt to be fair. They clearly play favorites, and open jealousy and rivalry occur quite naturally. In other cases, parents can cause rivalry without realizing it. When Beth Ann filled out her sibling survey questionnaire, she admitted she is still rivals with her older sister: "Almost everything is in competition—who has the cleaner house, etc." Beth Ann admits she was her mother's favorite child while her sister, Jennie, was Dad's favorite, but she still seems to think that her sister got the better deal, sometimes receiving favoritism from both parents.

She said one of the childhood memories that sticks most stubbornly in her mind was the time that, "my sister made the cheerleading team and my parents made such a big deal over it. I don't ever remember their doing anything like that for me and I felt sad and jealous."

Today Beth Ann wishes the rivalry would end. On the back of her questionnaire, in a hypothetical letter she wrote to her sister, she said:

I don't care how clean your house is or how much you spend on decorating. You have my approval no matter what. I love you very much and just want to be friends.

As I analyze Beth Ann's note to her sister, it is obvious she's looking for her sister's approval and probably the approval of many other people as well, including her parents. It's difficult to be sure that Beth Ann's parents really did favor her sister over her. All we have to go on is the cheerleading incident, but it's still true that when parents get excited over one child's success, they can set up competition between that child and other siblings even if they don't mean to.

ANYONE CAN HAVE SIBLING PROBLEMS

What parents tend to forget is that insecurity and jealousy are always lurking just under the surface with siblings. And in some cases the stakes are a lot higher than someone's success as a cheerleader. Thomas J. Watson, Jr., who served as chief executive officer of IBM from 1956 to 1971, wrote in his autobiography of feeling upset when it looked to him at one point as if his father were about to "hand over half of IBM" to his brother Dick. Watson writes:

> For years, before I had any successes of my own, the idea of Dick getting ahead really bothered me. Even though he was five years younger, I thought he was in many ways my superior. He'd gotten into Yale, and his grades were a . . . lot better than mine had been in college. He was a better athlete. He had a better command of languages and an easier way of relating to other people—he was much more gracious, a relaxed guy, very charming. He could sing and he could yodel, and he was a real entertainer at parties. Seeing Dick do so well had made me feel like the black sheep, and I thought people admired him because he lived up to what Dad wanted, and I didn't.[6]

Watson goes on to say that while he had great ambitions for himself he always felt warmly toward his brother and wanted him to succeed too. His real problems lay with his father, who had dreams of seeing both his boys running IBM together. In an attempt to bring Dick along a little faster so he could catch up to his older brother, Thomas Watson, Sr., created feelings of rivalry and competition between his sons that became a continuing problem in their business relationships, even though their private and social lives remained on a friendly basis.[7]

FAIR TREATMENT THAT BACKFIRES

The struggles between Thomas Watson, Jr., and his brother Dick at IBM illustrate an irony that I see repeating itself in many families as parents try to treat all their children as equals and be sure "everything is fair." In reality, they only set up competition between their children, who don't think they are being treated fairly at all!

Nancy, second-born among five brothers and sisters, always remembers rivalry and tension with her big sister, Alice, the first-born of the family. They were polar opposites from birth, particularly in the area of personal grooming. Nancy was neat while Alice was a mess.

As we talked, Nancy recalled: "Now that we're both grown and have families of our own, my mother tells me how she used to laugh when she saw us walking home from school together. Alice's hair was disheveled, her shirt wasn't tucked in, her knee-highs would be down around her ankles, and her shoes would be all dirty. My hair was in place, my knee-highs pulled up, my shirt tucked in, and my shoes were clean."

Today, Nancy confesses that she wishes she could "last an hour" in the same room with Alice. As Nancy and I continued to talk, it became clear that the girls grew up under the critical eye of perfectionistic parents, particularly their mother, who put a lot of stock in being neat. Born just a little over a year apart, the two girls became very, very competitive and in some ways Nancy displaced Alice and took over the first-born role.

When I asked Nancy if her parents always treated her and her sister the same, she said, "Oh, yes. They always strove to be fair. One of the things I can recall as a small child is my mother putting glasses on the table for all of us, and pouring out the Pepsi and making sure we all got exactly the same amount. No glass would have one millimeter more than another."

I pointed out to Nancy that if her mother had placed less importance on being exactly fair, she would have actually taught her children to be more generous and have a more sharing attitude. Being sure that "I get my share" is part of the scarcity mentality that encourages greed, not real sharing. Nancy's story is one of many I hear from siblings who were treated so fairly that, ironically, the treatment really bred the scarcity mentality of "I've got to look out for myself."

Today, as adults, Nancy and Alice are still rivals. Nancy's children are neat and well groomed while Alice's are messy. And while they live less than fifty miles apart, their families seldom get together. When they do get together, there is an atmosphere of comparing to see who has gotten what and which children have made the most progress in school, etc. The scarcity mentality is still at work.

JEALOUSY OF "GOODY TWO-SHOES"

Sometimes intense rivalry and a feeling on the part of one sibling that "Mom always liked you best" occurs when a brother or sister takes on the role of "goody two-shoes." This happened with Rebecca, first-born of six siblings, who still has serious tensions with her sister Janet, one year younger. Rebecca doesn't recall being treated "best" at all, but she does admit that she grew up as the "really straight one" in the family.

"I was always a good kid," she recalled. "I did my homework, kept my room clean, and never talked back to my parents. I didn't smoke or drink either. I was what my brothers and sisters called a prude, but that's not what I wanted to be. I just wanted to live right." She recalled that Janet, the sister directly below her, "always thought I was too perfect, too good. There was always something there. I always knew she had something against me as we were growing up."

Those feelings persist today for some ironic reasons because the story of Rebecca and Janet has an interesting twist. Although she played the role of the goody-goody who wanted to be right while growing up, that didn't make her immune to temptation and mistakes. When she got pregnant as a teenager, her dad kicked her out of the house and she married into an abusive situation that eventually led to divorce, much to the utter chagrin and horror of her Catholic parents and particularly her sister Janet.

Rebecca's divorce did not lessen Janet's feeling of jealousy toward her; in fact, it only increased the tension. Instead of being supportive of her sister, Janet put Rebecca down and told her, "You've got it made . . . you've got a beautiful house.

. . . What are you getting divorced for?" Rebecca replied that there are more things in life than living empty-hearted in a beautiful house and that she and her kids were really suffering, but Janet's disdain continued.

Later, when Rebecca remarried and she and her husband became born-again Christians, the screws of tension turned once again. Now Janet sees Rebecca even more as the goody two-shoes. When the sisters get together, Rebecca said she feels, "like I'm walking on egg shells with her. I don't want to say the wrong thing . . . I don't want to sound self-righteous. I just want to reach out and say, 'I'm still your sister and I love you.' "

But Rebecca finds it impossible to do this. Recently she got her sister to go to breakfast after having numerous invitations rebuffed. She wanted to reach out, but she felt resistance across the table and she just couldn't do it. The sisters did hug before they parted, which was at least a start, but they have a long way to go to mend the gap that has widened between them over the years.

THREE RACEHORSES

As siblings tell their stories of competition and jealousy, it's clear that when children are small, parents prepare the field but their children are the ones who play on it. As I look back on my childhood and how Warren, Larry, and I were reared by my parents, I have basically nothing but good memories of being loved—and treated fairly. But despite all that fair treatment, competition did arise. In a recent conversation about our sibling relationships, Larry drew an apropos analogy comparing the three Carlson brothers to three racehorses.

Warren, the oldest, broke out of the chute first and had the inside lane. Six years later, Larry came down the track in the middle lane, and finally, five years after that, Randy got his chance to break from the starting gate, winding up in the outside lane, where he had to run a lot faster to catch up with his older brothers.

As I thought about Larry's racehorse analogy, it became clear that when we were young, I was the one who did most of the competing. No one told me I had to run faster. My parents, in particular, never urged me to compete with or try to catch up to my older brothers. Through my own private logic, I decided to do that on my own.

Later, as we became adults, we all ran our own race on different tracks. Warren went into the corporate world of the health-care field. Larry took over the Youth Haven Ranch ministry he had co-founded with our parents, and I went into radio and marriage/family counseling. But while we all ran on different tracks, we all worked hard to fulfill the family motto, which we learned from both our parents, but mainly from my dad:

Work hard, serve faithfully, and never say no.

Those words sum up Morry Carlson's life, and he has been a working model for his three sons to follow. All of us have concentrated on working hard to serve God and our fellow man, and because we are so oriented to helping others, we find it difficult to say no, even when we should. Our family motto also helps explain why all of us have sometimes been too busy to be sufficiently interested in one another. The strengths of our family motto have turned into a weakness that we all need to be aware of and correct.

As I try to analyze who might have been the "favorite" among us, I can't come up with a clear-cut candidate, and perhaps that's the way our parents planned it. True, first-born Warren got more "toys" than Larry and I did, particularly in the form of cars. Through high school he had two or three cars, which were financed at least in part by my folks. I can remember him driving off on dates in his '57 Ford and his Nash Metropolitan, a forerunner of today's tiny subcompacts.

Second-born Larry probably felt like the least favorite (most middle children do). I'm sure, for example, having to move back and forth between Warren's room and my room didn't help. As for me, the baby of the family, I did my best to manipulate Mom and Dad to help me survive the teasing of my big brothers when I was little, but once I got into grade school, they more or less went their way and I went mine. I can only conclude that there was no clear-cut favorite among the Carlson boys, but there was competition, mainly on my part, and that syndrome continues today.

THE FAMILY MOTTO

Most family mottoes are unspoken; they operate within the family on a subconscious level. Healthy family mottoes motivate siblings toward pursuing excellence but not perfectionism. Unhealthy mottoes motivate siblings to engage in destructive competition, rivalry, and conflict.

Family mottoes are as varied as families, but like life roles, they can be grouped under general headings. Look at the following family mottoes and see if any of them represents the one you grew up with. Check the one (or perhaps more than one) that applies:

Family Mottoes

____ "Only your best is good enough." In this family the kids are supposed to shape up and perform because performance is everything. What they accomplish gives them status and acceptance in the family. How one looks to others is all-important. Acceptance or rejection is based on bringing honor or disgrace to the family.

____ "Take care; don't take any chances." This is the motto of the cautious family that teaches the children they you can never be too careful because the world is a risky place.

____ "He who dies with the most toys wins." This well-known bumper sticker has been the motto of many families where material things and having a good time are really important and people run a distant second. Many families live unconsciously by this motto although they'd never admit it.

____ "Don't let the grass grow under your feet." In this family the message is to grow up fast and to live and play hard. Life isn't something to watch; it's something to do. And the faster the pace you set, the better.

____ "Only the strong survive." This is one of the most competitive of all family mottoes because it teaches each child that he or she must go all out to beat everybody else.

____ "Hard work is your key to success." One of the most common of family mottoes among Americans, this is seldom com-

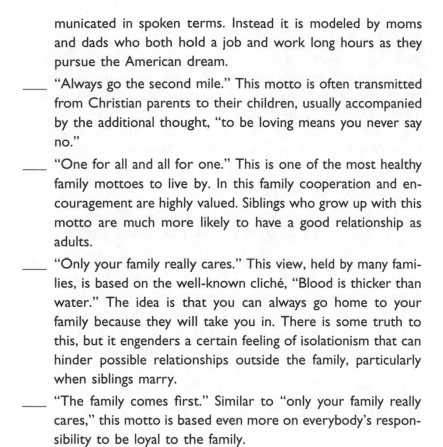

municated in spoken terms. Instead it is modeled by moms and dads who both hold a job and work long hours as they pursue the American dream.

_____ "Always go the second mile." This motto is often transmitted from Christian parents to their children, usually accompanied by the additional thought, "to be loving means you never say no."

_____ "One for all and all for one." This is one of the most healthy family mottoes to live by. In this family cooperation and encouragement are highly valued. Siblings who grow up with this motto are much more likely to have a good relationship as adults.

_____ "Only your family really cares." This view, held by many families, is based on the well-known cliché, "Blood is thicker than water." The idea is that you can always go home to your family because they will take you in. There is some truth to this, but it engenders a certain feeling of isolationism that can hinder possible relationships outside the family, particularly when siblings marry.

_____ "The family comes first." Similar to "only your family really cares," this motto is based even more on everybody's responsibility to be loyal to the family.

You may have found your family motto in the above list, or it may have been necessary for you to combine parts of two or more statements to best describe your family. The question is, are you still adhering to your family motto? As siblings grow up and move out of their family of origin, they may take the family motto along or they may leave it behind. A good rule of thumb is that siblings who cling to unhealthy family mottoes experience dissatisfaction when they try to relate to each other as adults. In contrast, siblings who embrace healthy family mottoes stand a much better chance of having a good relationship as adults.

Siblings who embrace healthy family mottoes stand a much better chance of having a good relationship as adults.

Another important issue is what happens to the family motto when a sibling marries. Typically, when you marry you blend your family motto with your spouse's family motto and come up with your own new family motto. Sometimes this works out nicely, but in other cases when another sibling has married and a new motto has come out of that union, your new motto and his or her new motto may clash and cause tension and problems. In Chapter 9 we'll look further at what can happen to sibling relationships after siblings marry and start families of their own.

WHERE DO WE GO FROM HERE?

In these first five chapters, we have been looking at adult sibling rivalry through the lens of "the problem." Perhaps you have seen yourself quite clearly in one or more of the examples I've described, including my own relationship to my brothers. It's also quite possible that you haven't seen yourself because your situation is quite different from any of the examples used so far. It's fairly safe to say, however, that you're probably among the 90-plus percent of people who say they want their relationships to their siblings to be better. And that means that right now you are facing some level of sibling rivalry:

- You may have open conflict with or hatred for siblings. You can't stand to be in the same room together more than five minutes, and every Christmas reunion usually turns into a war.

- You may have a so-so relationship that remains calm on the surface as long as you don't get too close or stay together too long, but, like Mount Saint Helens, trouble is bubbling just beneath the apparent calm.

- You may just be indifferent, seldom seeing each other and, until now, not really caring too much.

- You may have a fairly good relationship, but because you battle hang-ups from the past, you still experience frustration and a longing to go deeper, open up a little more, or just know each other better.

Whatever the level of your sibling tensions may be, it's quite possible that there are feelings of lack of respect on someone's part. Perhaps the issues go back to certain memories of what it was like to be in the family atmosphere, born at a certain place, and the player of a certain role in the family.

Perhaps you're quite ready to admit the green-eyed monster of jealousy is a big part of your present problem; on the other hand, you may think the term *jealousy* doesn't quite fit. Somewhere along the line, however, you and your sibling may have competed to some degree, and maybe that competition is still going on and needs some squaring away.

In Part 2 of this book, we'll switch from the problem lens to the positive lens and look at different aspects of how to improve your sibling relationships. You may have a lot of work to do to even establish communication, or you may be at the other end of the spectrum where you already have good communication and would just like to fine-tune something that has been going along pretty well. Wherever you are on the continuum, the principles and tools in the following chapters will help you improve your adult sibling relationships.

We'll start by examining some positive sibling situations. Believe it or not, there are actually siblings who have no rivalry. What do such good sibling relationships look like? What are the elements that enable sibs to interact well, to not feel jealousy or rivalry, and to always be there for one another? In Chapter 6 we'll meet siblings, some unknown and some famous, who have been able to enjoy warm and even intimate bonds throughout their lives.

Part 2

How to Defeat the Cain and Abel Syndrome

(and what to do if you can't)

Chapter 6

THE SECRETS TO BEING CLOSE TO YOUR SIBLINGS

In Part 1, we looked at key reasons why many siblings have rivalry of some kind. At best, this kind of relationship isn't all that at least one sibling wishes it could be. There are, however, siblings who do get along beautifully as adults. They genuinely like each other and feel no rivalry at all. Why? What makes them different?

As I surveyed and researched adult siblings from all walks of life, there seemed to be a basic quality to every warm sibling relationship that could best be called a sense of unity or family. In her autobiography *Get to the Heart*, singing star Barbara Mandrell put it this way:

> From the moment we were put together on this earth, we became a unit. The Mandrell Sisters. We might quarrel over

a game or an item of clothing, but we never had any natural pairings, any two-against-one stuff. I think if Daddy and Mama had caught us taking sides, they would have busted all three of us. Sisters stick together.[1]

It doesn't take much reading between the lines to deduce that the Mandrell parents were wise, loving—and firm. They didn't play favorites and they allowed no cliques, no ganging up by one pair of sisters on the third. The result was "a unit."

Barbara Mandrell had five years of being an only child before her parents started letting her know a new baby was on the way. Mr. and Mrs. Mandrell were probably not familiar with the psychological term *displacement,* but instinctively they knew that their daughter might feel shoved aside when a new baby started attracting all the attention. So they tried to explain to Barbara that people had been caring for her, and now it was her turn to do some caring for baby sister. But somehow Daddy, in particular, wasn't totally convinced that Barbara was all that happy about the soon-to-be blessed event.

When Daddy brought Mama and the new baby home, he exclaimed to five-year-old Barbara, "They gave me the wrong baby! Look at all this black hair. This is not my baby!" Then ominously proclaiming that he was going to "flush the baby away," he took her in the bathroom, shut the door, and flushed the toilet. Distressed, five-year-old Barbara jerked open the door and there was her new baby sister safe and sound with Daddy. Looking back on the incident, Barbara recalled:

Daddy had just been teasing me. It sounds kind of crude and cruel the way we tell it, but it had the desired effect. From that moment on, she was my baby, too. . . . From that moment, Daddy knew that I was part of the team. I was fiercely protective of my sisters, the way my parents had been of me.[2]

THE KEY TO LESS SIBLING RIVALRY

While some might quibble with Daddy Mandrell's technique, he got the result he was looking for: His oldest child developed a sense of ownership in her younger siblings that she carried with her all her life. The imagery of being "part of the team" is also noteworthy. If more families saw themselves as a team working together, there would be much less sibling rivalry as children or into adulthood.

Whenever siblings have a positive, almost-ideal relationship, certain forces pull them together: Similar goals, a crisis or tragedy, mutual suffering, or some kind of shared talents, abilities, or interest. People who have a warm, positive, adult sibling relationship usually recall a certain time or perhaps a particular event when they bonded with their brothers or sisters. For Barbara Mandrell at least one of these telling moments came when Daddy threatened to "flush her baby sister away" and Barbara rushed to protect her sibling. This is a refreshing change from so many kids who would be the first to reach for the toilet handle!

In the long run, parents usually get what they expect. Mom and Dad Mandrell expected their children to have unity, to work together, and to be part of a team. Then—and this is all-important—they followed through to make it happen.

Barbara's parents named their second child Thelma Louise and less than two years later one more sister arrived—Ellen Irlene. Barbara quickly became supreme leader of the group, taking charge almost automatically to guide her siblings in everything from playing in tree houses to caroling at Christmas to putting on little shows in the living room. She recalled:

> I was the formidable one, the leader; they looked up to me. I was rarely hurt. I was indestructible. I never felt any responsibility or pressure to be the leader, I just was. I was the oldest. . . . Sometimes I find it impossible to explain to people how close we three girls always have been. I always had this idealistic, fairy-tale belief that all brothers and sisters are so close, and all parents and children are so close.[3]

The same feeling of family unity shows up in Kathryn Hepburn's book *Me: Stories of My Life*:

> We were close and we are still close. . . . We're sort of a "group" going through the world together. Isn't that won-

derful? I feel so lucky. I feel cared for and I have always felt cared for.[4]

One of the strongest sibling teams I came across in my research was Wilbur and Orville Wright, whose accomplishments at Kitty Hawk, North Carolina, on December 17, 1903, opened the age of flight. Born five years apart as fifth and sixth in a family of seven children, Wilbur and Orville came from a strong, stable family headed by their father, Milton, a bishop in the Church of the United Brethren in Christ. Both brothers remained bachelors all their lives, but they never lacked for friends or staunch supporters, particularly in their own family circle. One biographer of the Wright Brothers wrote:

> The world looked at these two men and saw a corporate entity: the Wright Brothers. Indeed, their ability to function as a team was nothing short of extraordinary. Their father had once told a reporter they were "as inseparable as twins." Perhaps so, but they remained very different men. They understood that fact—it was one of the secrets of their success. Each of them was prepared to rely on the other's strengths and to compensate for his weaknesses.[5]

The family motto for the Mandrells, the Hepburns, or the Wrights could easily have been "one for all and all for one." The feeling of belonging to one another and being responsible for one another runs throughout their stories. Whenever there is a good connection between siblings that lasts into adulthood, you usually find that sense of protecting one another, caring for one another, and being happy for each other's successes. Well-connected siblings are there for each other in failure or tragedy, and they work as a team. If one sibling hurts, the other one does also. If one sibling is happy, so is the other one.

Well-connected siblings . . . work as a team.

FOUR REASONS FOR FAMILY UNITY

At least four key reasons create an attitude of "one for all and all for one" among siblings:

- Loving parents who built a strong relationship with their children.
- Good communication skills.
- The ability to solve conflicts and difficulties together.
- A great deal of positive time spent together.

As I mentioned earlier, parents prepare the ground on which their siblings play the game of life. Some parents do it much better than others and the results are obvious. When speaking of her own parents, Kathryn Hepburn wrote glowingly:

What can I say? The luck of having Dad and Mother. They really loved each other. . . . They took what life had to offer and they gobbled it up. Some send off. A real set of values—and a sense of joy . . . we were a happy family. We are a happy family. Mother and Dad were perfect parents. They brought us up with a feeling of freedom. There were NO RULES. There were simply certain things which we did—and certain things which we didn't do because they would hurt others.[6]

The same strong sense of parental love also comes through in the Wright biography. Wilbur, Orville, and their five brothers and sisters had their squabbles, as all siblings do. There was an occasional need for discipline that included spankings, but the basic atmosphere in the Wright home was one of love and affection. Milton Wright and his wife, Susan, ". . . were warm, loving, and protective parents who encouraged a close relationship between their children."[7]

The influence of parents—positive or negative—can never be denied. In one case, a man with four brothers and two sisters, all living within 250 miles of each other, shared during a sibling seminar that he enjoyed the company of his siblings whenever they all got together and has never felt rivalry with any of them. He added:

I would commend the parents who raised us. Dad, because he showed us how to work and the importance of being a good worker. Mom, because of her faith and faithfulness in giving us her best. Because of this, I would say we enjoy a healthy relationship as siblings that is a reminder to try to raise our children in a similar fashion.

COMMUNICATION: OVERWORKED WORD, UNDEVELOPED SKILL

While *communication* is an overworked word, it is also an un-developed skill in too many families. Happy sibs, however, seem to communicate very well. During a siblings seminar I conducted, one brother wrote this hypothetical letter to his younger brother to express how he felt about their relationship:

Dear Bob,

It's with great joy and pleasure that I think of how our relationship has grown. I enjoy the mutual respect and openness that we share. I also appreciate the fact that we can talk about deep and difficult subjects, at times disagreeing in our viewpoints, and still learn from each other and have a beneficial conversation.

So good were the Wright Brothers' communication and ability to solve their problems that they even enjoyed an occasional argument or "fight." Wilbur once said he loved to argue with Orville because he was such a "good scrapper." They could argue in such a way that it was like "tossing ideas back and forth in a kind of verbal shorthand until a kernel of truth began to emerge. Their ability to argue through to a solution of a prob-lem would prove very useful to them."[8]

Good communication and an ability to solve problems and work through conflicts doesn't happen unless plenty of positive time is spent together. From childhood, the Wright brothers were almost inseparable. More than four years older than Orville, Wilbur became his brother's protector and guide. He told him stories, taught him to build kites, and was in every sense "unofficial guide and advisor" to Orville and his friends. In his will, prepared shortly before he died in 1912, Wilbur said of his brother that they had been "associated . . . in all hopes and labors, both of childhood and manhood."[9]

BLESSING ONE ANOTHER

Siblings who have a close and positive relationship throughout their lives all seem to know instinctively how to bless one another in warm and specific ways. Most families may know little of the biblical kind of blessing mentioned in the story of Isaac and his sons Jacob and Esau. Nonetheless, they have the natural ability to unconditionally accept one another and meet each other's needs for intimacy and affection. They know how to touch one another in ways that make them feel supported, loved—and blessed.

Siblings who have a close and positive relationship . . . know instinctively how to bless one another in warm and specific ways.

One of the best descriptions of communicating these feelings of warmth, love, and support that I have found is in the fine book *The Gift of the Blessing*, which was co-authored by my good friend and colleague Dr. John Trent, who finds time out of his busy counseling duties to sit on our board at "Today's Family Life." John and his co-author, Gary Smalley, wrote *The Gift of the Blessing* with parents and children primarily in mind, because their counseling work put them in touch with so many people who had come from homes devoid of the blessing. In speaking of this genuine acceptance, Smalley and Trent describe it as:

> a need that goes unmet in thousands of lives today—perhaps you have this need or a loved one is struggling with it, a need that the blessing helps to meet. Yet, the family blessing not only provides people a much needed sense of personal acceptance, it also plays an important part in protecting and even freeing them to develop intimate relationships.[11]

Personal stories shared by my clients and callers to "Parent Talk" verify that Smalley and Trent are correct, but their concept of the blessing can go far beyond parents and children. The benefits of blessing others can be transferred easily to any intimate relationship: between husbands and wives, between friends, between church members—and, yes, between siblings.

According to Smalley and Trent, the blessing includes five key elements, all of which apply quite directly to improving relationships with an adult sibling, or anyone else for that matter. These five elements are:

- Meaningful touch.
- A spoken or written message of love and concern.
- Letting the one being blessed know that he or she has high value.
- Letting the one being blessed know that he or she has a special future.
- Fulfilling the blessing through an active commitment of your time and resources.[12]

I believe that if these five elements were a regular part of an adult sibling relationship, there would be NO rivalry—period. A brief look at each of these five elements tells us why:

It takes eight to ten "meaningful touches" daily to maintain proper emotional and physical health.

Meaningful touch is so important that one recent research study found that it takes eight to ten "meaningful touches" daily to maintain proper emotional and physical health. In my counseling work I am continually amazed to learn of people, many from Christian homes, who grew up lacking meaningful touches from their parents or their siblings. For many, the only touches they got from a sibling were punches, kicks, or pinches.

For other people, meaningful touches were limited. They were hugged and physically loved in their early years, but as early as grade school, the hugs stopped. It's as if parents think, *Oh, he's too big for hugs now; besides he doesn't like them,* or *It will embarrass her if I hug her in front of her friends.* The fact is, kids (and adults) of all ages need hugs and meaningful touches.

To meaningfully touch a child or a teenager or even an adult sibling doesn't require a ten-minute, bone-crushing embrace. Sometimes it just means an affectionate pat on the shoulder or a squeeze of the hand. It is no coincidence that studies have shown that touching has physiological benefits. One researcher made numerous studies on the effects of the practice many Christians recognize called "laying on of hands." She discovered that when one person lays hands on another, the hemoglobin levels in the bloodstreams of both people go up, which means that body tissues receive more oxygen, producing more energy and even regenerative power.[13]

It's doubtful that your sibling thinks much about hemoglobin levels when you touch him or her, but what he or she does think about is the fact that you really care.

The spoken or written word is another powerful conveyor of blessing to your sibling, particularly when you communicate that you are proud of or grateful to a brother or sister. In one seminar I conducted, a young woman wrote to her older sister saying:

> I thank God for giving me such a wonderful sister and friend! You have always made me feel worthwhile because you are always willing to listen to me, and you don't try to hide anything from me. If I didn't have you as a sister, I don't think I would have made it through my childhood.

Expressing such powerful words of blessing to your sibling may be difficult to do face-to-face. Keep in mind that there are other obvious ways to communicate, such as over the phone or through the mail. One of the long-distance telephone companies made famous the line, "Reach out and touch someone." Those are perhaps five of the most powerful words ever put into a TV commercial. And the reason they have such power is that people instinctively want to be touched. You want it, I want it, and our siblings want it.

Attaching high value to someone means you let them know they are very important to you. The root meaning of the word *blessing* means "to bow the knee." You don't bow before someone or some thing to which you give little value. Instead, you treat this person or object with honor and respect.

Smalley and Trent believe the best way to communicate a message of high value with anyone is to draw a "word picture" that describes that person's qualities or character traits *apart from his or her performance.* So often in families we hesitate to praise or encourage anyone unless he or she has accomplished something. The result is that family members may feel they're loved only for what they can do, not for who they are.

The idea behind letting your sibling know that he or she has great value in your eyes is that you want to say something simple that conveys how special he or she is to you. In a way, that is what Kathryn Hepburn does when she writes of her brothers and sisters:

> I cannot say anything in detail about my sisters and brothers. They are such a part of me that I simply know that I could not have been me without them. They are my "box" —my protection.[14]

In that word *box*, Kathryn Hepburn paints a word picture that says more than a thousand words. Her brothers and sisters were her fortress of protection, and she has felt that way right into her eighties.

What word picture could you use to convey to your sibling that you hold him or her in high value or esteem? Perhaps your sibling has been a "rock" to whom you can cling and upon whom you can depend. Or perhaps when you think of your sibling, you picture "dropping a bucket in the well and always coming up with cold, fresh water."

Another approach to a word picture is to use a simple nickname like "Big Sister," which is what Barbara Mandrell's younger siblings called her throughout childhood because she was so much older and so definitely their leader.

The descriptive words you can use to attach high value to your sibling are practically innumerable. On the other hand, you may not feel very adept at coining nicknames or using metaphors or similes. In that case you can simply tell your sibling, "You are very special and valuable to me." That's what Juanita did during a sibling seminar when she recalled a sister who was always there for her while she suffered a physical handicap that kept her in and out of hospitals for the first eighteen years of her life. The fourth of six children, Juanita remembered that her older sister not only helped her battle her physical handicap but also those terrible feelings of being unwanted. On her questionnaire, Juanita wrote:

To my special sister, who always took the time to visit me almost every day in the hospital: On my birthday you brought me a watch and a birthday cake with a huge candle in the center. You made sure I had a television set and a radio so that the time I spent in a body cast would pass more quickly.

Maria's loving care and concern is the one bright spot that helps Juanita block out those early memories of being bedridden and feeling unwanted. Her sister's love and attention were like a healing medicine for her soul, and she carries that memory with her today.

Picturing a special future for someone is another way of saying, "Always give encouragement." Here especially the power of words is all-important. Parents who tell their children, "You're lazy" or "you're stupid" or "you're mean" or "you're a smart aleck" are simply pronouncing what can be self-fulfilling prophesies.

And the same is true with our siblings. Realize that any time you communicate with a sibling, whatever you say is essentially going to accomplish one of two things: encouraging your brother or sister or discouraging him or her. Listen to your siblings talk about their goals and dreams, then feed that back to them with comments like, "You can do it . . . you have the talent and the guts . . . you are always such an example to me."

Listen to your siblings talk about their goals and dreams, then feed that back to them with comments like, "You can do it." . . .

In so many families, the prevailing atmosphere is one of criticism, censure, disagreement, quibbling, and destructive teasing or joking done under the guise of "just kidding." Praise and encouragement are doled out grudgingly as if family members think they are going to spoil someone or give him or her a reason to be conceited. The truth is, in almost all families there is seldom enough encouragement—those good and pleasant words that build up, inspire, and comfort.

In Barbara Mandrell's family, however, encouragement and support abound. In her biography, she wrote:

To this day, I depend on my sisters for love and guidance. I talk with Irlene almost every day when I am home in Nashville, and Louise and I share messages on yellow legal pads. We both rely on each other to criticize our shows. If we don't help each other, who will?[15]

An active commitment to blessing your sibling means actually doing something to communicate your love and devotion. As powerful as words are, they need to be backed up by actions if you are totally serious about blessing those you love.

Commitment translated into action is beautifully illustrated by author John Trent's mother, who committed herself to her three sons in a very specific fashion. If you were to visit her home, you would find a bookshelf with one section filled with theology and psychology books (John's major interest in life). In another section are medical journals and books on genetics, the major interests of John's brother Jeff, who specializes in cancer research. Not only did Mom try to learn how to read medical and genetics books that were practically incomprehensible to a layperson, but at the age of sixty, she even took a beginning genetics class at a local college. That she had to drop the course after failing the first two major exams is not the point. She was willing to *try* to learn about her son's profession and in so doing she communicated a blessing to him.

And what about John's other brother, Joe? He is represented on that same bookshelf by copies of *Heavy Equipment Digest*. For several years he excelled as a heavy-equipment operator, and his mother wanted to be able to talk about the latest bulldozer or earth mover that had just come on the market.[16]

Applying the same principle to your siblings shouldn't be too hard if you know what their major interests are and you're willing to learn more about them. Yes, it will take time, and your sibling's interests or hobbies may not interest you too much at all. You may have to become a student of the mysteries of hockey or basketball. Perhaps you will have to learn something about antiques, cooking, or fly-fishing. How personally appealing any of these topics or pastimes are is not the issue; they can be a way to know and bless your sibling better, and that's the real goal.

You Can't Fool a Sibling

Taking time to learn more about your sibling's interests and concerns is just one basic way to commit yourself to actions that bless his or her life. Even more important, perhaps, is simply being there. This means something a little bit different in every sibling relationship, but at the very heart of this issue is a willingness and a commitment to be involved in your sibling's life at those points and at those times that are most important to him or her. Siblings may botch things; siblings may neglect one another or talk out of turn and hurt each other's feelings. But when siblings know they can count on each another in the really tough times, they can go a long way together down whatever rocky road life brings.

Whenever possible, be there to help your sibling in person with whatever needs to be done. Or be there to listen when your sibling wants to talk about concerns or problems. If you can't be there in person, there is always the telephone.

> **Whenever possible, be there to help your sibling.**

Crucial questions we can ask ourselves are:

1. Will my siblings be there for me when they are needed?

2. Will I be there for my siblings when I am needed?

These questions don't have a lot to do with how perfect your sibling relationships may be. The bottom line, however, is an absolute commitment on the part of one sibling to another to be available in the good times and the bad, to rejoice together and to weep together. It may mean as little as a phone call or a card. It may mean a hug or a pat on the shoulder or a word of encouragement. At the other end of the spectrum, it may mean catching a red-eye flight on an hour's notice and flying across the country to be at your sibling's side. As one sister wrote to her older brother, "You have always been there for me and are still there. I love you for that!"

If you had to rate your commitment level to your siblings on a one-to-ten scale, with one being lowest and ten being highest, what would it be? Put down a number in the margin right now —and be honest. To paraphrase Josh McDowell's well-known saying, You can con a con, you can fool a fool, but you can't kid a kid—or your sibling.

When adult siblings have a truly warm and sound relationship, they constantly bless one another without effort or even without realizing it. Blessing one another is what they want to do, not what they have to do.

You may be thinking, *All this sounds great. I'd love to have sibling relationships like these, but when you ask about "being there," I'm not sure my siblings will even be there for my funeral. We grew up rivals and we're still rivals, so I guess I'm stuck.*

Not necessarily. There are ways to solve the rivalry riddle. We'll start looking at some specifics in Chapter 7.

Chapter 7

SOLVING THE RIVALRY RIDDLE

All right, suppose you're convinced you'd like to improve relationships with your sister or brother, but you're not sure how to go about it. Maybe your sibling lives in another state and you only see each other at Christmas or perhaps at a wedding or reunion that comes along every few years. Or it could be that you and your sib live in the same community so getting together more often wouldn't be too hard—*if* you could only bridge the emotional distance between the two of you.

In *Brothers and Sisters: How They Shape Our Lives*, Jane Leder ponders the difficulties some siblings might have in trying to reconnect. She observes that changing old patterns and navigating a relationship differently can feel as dangerous as walking through a mine field. She writes: "It can be extremely hard to form a new relationship with an adult sibling we don't really know any more or never really knew in the first place."[1]

No matter what your sibling situation, keep in mind that everything changes over time. No relationship is static. Your connection to your siblings is either getting stronger or weaker. You are either drawing closer, or you are moving further apart. You are either spending less time with each other or more time with each other.

If you are willing to spend the time and the effort . . . you and your sibling may actually become close.

If you fail to work on improving your sibling relationships, they will grow more distant and eventually strained, and in some cases they may even become hostile. But if you are willing to spend the time and effort, in most cases you can see positive results. You and your sibling may actually become close. If that's a lot to ask, perhaps you will learn to be much more at ease with one another. Or, in some cases, at least you'll be able to stay in the same room together at the next family reunion! (Chapter 11 includes suggestions for what to do if your efforts in this direction cause you to "hit a blank wall.")

Developing a Strategy

Set Realistic Goals. If you want to improve any sibling relationship, you need a strategy, a plan with goals that are realistic and reachable. Setting realistic goals for improving relationships with a sibling often means lowering your expectations of what you hope to accomplish. Don't forget the equation: Expectations minus reality equals disappointment. If your expectations are too high reality may easily dash your hopes, and you will be disappointed.

All of us have a tendency to fantasize the ideal relationships we'd like to have with our sibling: close, warm, and intimate, sharing the deepest secrets of our hearts, always being there for one another. In some cases, this ideal relationship can happen over time; for other sibs, the ideal relationship may not be reachable for any number of reasons. That doesn't mean, however, that you can't make things better—a lot better.

As you set goals, make them reachable; don't bite off more

than either of you can chew. Perhaps you could try to get together on a casual basis or try to have some fun together; but don't get into anything deep. Going over old hurts or sore points can come later.

Consider the Cost. In keeping your goals realistic and reachable, it makes good sense to count the cost versus the amount of possible return. Put your time and energy where you are likely to have the most success. Otherwise you may get discouraged, and no real changes will occur.

Choosing the Best Prospects. If there is distance between you and more than one sibling, your most realistic and reachable goal is to pick the sibling with whom you have the most potential for improving your relationship. For example, don't start with the black-sheep brother who is possibly an alcoholic, a drug addict, or doing time in jail. Instead, begin with that kid sister who was always a pest when you were younger but now is married and living not too far away with her husband and two kids.

I'm not suggesting that you abandon the alcoholic brother; you should never totally give up on any sibling. But reconnecting with siblings is not easy work, and it's usually better to begin where the ground is smoother. You can work up to the mountain climbing later.

Keep It Simple. When setting goals to improve relationships with a sibling, the most important question you can ask yourself is this:

What single thing would I like to see happen that would really improve things between me and my sibling?

This single thing should not be overly ambitious. A key part of your strategy can be described in a variation of the motto K.I.S.S. In this case, it's "keep it simple, sibling."

Equal Empowerment. If you try to get together with your sibling, be sure the conversation or the activity is something that will be comfortable for both of you. What you're after is "equal empowerment"—a level playing field, so to speak.

Too often when adult siblings get together they fall right back into the familiar pattern they knew as children. They find themselves communicating child-to-child, and naturally it's very easy to get into the same old wrangles and arguments. Or if one sibling played the role of father or mother figure for another sibling while growing up, that same old adult-to-child pattern can surface when they try to relate as adults, with the usual negative results.

Equal empowerment means an adult-to-adult relationship. You see yourself as an adult and you see your sibling as an adult as well.

Meet in a Neutral Spot. Another way to achieve equal empowerment is to meet in a neutral spot. If trouble always starts in a certain person's home or at a certain kind of gathering, avoid those settings. Try to get together on neutral ground —a restaurant, a park, a friend's house—whatever is comfortable for both of you.

And when you do get together, have some neutral but interesting topics ready to discuss. Avoid subjects that you know can be provocative or even volatile. Keep in mind, too, that everyone likes to be asked about his or her life and interests; few people like to hear *only* about yours.

PUTTING THE PRINCIPLES TO WORK

To see how these principles work, let's apply them to Ruth, who stepped up to talk to me after I had taught a seminar on siblings. A middle child, she had sibling problems with her older sister Lois and her "black-sheep" baby sister Sarah, as well as her baby brother Mark, who had formed an alliance with Lois and had avoided Ruth as much as possible over the years.

The bottom line was that Ruth was not really close to her two sisters and her brother. When I asked her why, she said she believed it went back to their childhood when she became her parents' favorite because she was compliant and easy to get along with. Right from the beginning, first-born Lois had always bumped heads with Daddy. When Ruth came along later, she quickly grew into the goody two-shoes of the family. She never gave her parents any trouble, got good grades, was clean and tidy, and as she grew up, she was always home on time from dates. In contrast, Lois always struggled in school, never did her chores, and was usually late coming home from dates.

"When the younger sibling replaces the first-born as the one who is more capable or more approved of, we call it *displacement*," I commented. "It sounds as if this is what might have happened with you and Lois."

"I guess you could call it that. At least I became the more 'accepted' of the two of us, and then when my younger sister, Sarah, turned into a total rebel, that pretty well clinched it."

Four years younger than Ruth, Sarah was a combination baby princess and tomboy, and she became her dad's favorite—until Mark came along. When Daddy finally got his "real boy," that knocked Sarah off her pedestal and in the years that followed, she bumped heads with her father more than Lois ever had. In high school Sarah started running with the wrong crowd and soon was into alcohol, drugs, and sleeping around. By the time she was nineteen, she had had two abortions.

Sarah finally left home and moved back to the East Coast to live with one of her uncles. Ruth had stayed in touch with Sarah, mostly by letter, and their correspondence was a record of the younger sister's downward spiral. Today Sarah is twenty-seven and on her third live-in relationship. She's trying to stay off drugs but she still drinks too much, and recently she attempted suicide and wound up in a psychiatric hospital.

As for Mark, he stayed out of trouble, and after graduating from high school, got married and moved several states away. No one hears from him except Lois, who was his second mother of sorts, as he grew. Lois and Mark would often band together to give Ruth a hard time or try to make her look bad in front of her parents, but it seldom worked because Ruth was "the apple of their eye."

Close-Range Rivals. Today Ruth and Lois both live in the same community. Both are married with children; Ruth has two and Lois has four.

"Lois reminds me quite often that I only have two kids," Ruth said. "I always have to explain that two is plenty for someone with a school-teaching career. I teach sixth grade and my husband is a high school principal."

Lois, she said, "would like to stay home with her kids, but her husband is a produce manager in a supermarket here in town and doesn't make a lot of money, so she has to work part-time as a secretary for a construction company. That drives a wedge between us, too, because she sees me as having it made while she's saddled with four kids and having to work to boot."

I said, "Let me see if I have the picture: You live in the same community with your older sister, Lois, but you don't have much of a relationship with her. You seldom see your younger sister, Sarah, anymore because she lives at the other end of the country, but you do write now and then. And Mark lives in another state and you seldom hear from him although he does keep in touch with Lois."

Ruth nodded. "That's about it. I used to write to Sarah quite often and her letters back to me would be filled with anger and hostility toward Mom and Dad, particularly Daddy. I feel badly about Sarah—as her older sister, maybe I should have done more to save her. I think I let her slip through the cracks."

Deciding Where to Start. Ruth wanted to have better relationships with all her siblings, but she didn't quite know where to start. She felt bad about outdoing her older sister and she also felt responsible for her younger sister, Sarah, almost blaming herself because Sarah had become the black sheep of the family. In fact, she admitted to me that she worried the most about Sarah because she had the most problems.

I told Ruth her first target should be Lois, who was living right in her community, and despite the competitive feelings that Lois especially had, the gap there was smaller than between Ruth and her other siblings. Ruth was willing to try to mend fences with Lois, but she wasn't optimistic because past "obligatory holiday get-togethers" or occasional efforts on Ruth's part to have Lois and her family for dinner had always ended in tension and remarks about Ruth having it made and how Lois always had to struggle.

"Tell me, Ruth," I asked, "what single thing would you like to see happen that would really improve things between you and Lois?"

"I guess I'd just wish we could be better friends," Ruth said slowly. "I've never really tried to outdo Lois and it wasn't my fault that she bumped heads with Daddy so much. I just wish we could get together and not have so much tension and competition."

"Do you ever try to get together with Lois one-on-one?"

"Not really. We're both pretty busy with jobs and families."

"I think that's where I'd start. Try to find an area where you have something in common, then invite Lois to get together with you to explore that area. Maybe you both like decorating or painting or shopping . . ."

"Now that you mention it, we both like antiques. Mom got us started with those and we both picked up on it."

"Then why not plan a day when you can both get away for lunch and do a little antique shopping?" I suggested. "Keep it all low key and don't get into any heavy conversations, particularly about your parents. I think one of your first goals is to get Lois to let her guard down. She sees you as the one who has made it with a career you love and a husband who is a successful leader in the community. She's the one having to scramble to raise four kids while you only have two, and she thinks it's much easier. Let her know you have your problems, too, that you're not perfect, and you have struggles and questions like everyone else. If possible, ask her advice on things like parenting or decorating or which antique to buy. Go very slow and see what happens."

"I suppose we could get together on a Saturday. Our husbands could baby-sit for a few hours. I'll call her and try to set it up."

"Great! I'd love to hear what happens, and there's one more thing—remember that you're trying to change something that took years to form. The tensions you feel with your sister go all the way back to when you were kids. The two of you probably aren't going to become warm, bosom buddies after one or two lunches and prowling a couple of antique stores together. Set your goals high but not too high. Be realistic and don't expect instant success. That way if Lois just isn't interested in getting together, you won't be too disappointed, and if you do make some progress it will be a special victory."

I didn't hear from Ruth for almost two months, and I began to think she had decided to forget the whole thing, but one day she called with a new enthusiasm in her voice that I hadn't heard the night we had chatted following the seminar. Yes, she had called her older sister and, strangely enough, she had sounded almost flattered to be invited to lunch and go antique shopping. They'd been out several times in the last few weeks, and while Lois still had some basic misperceptions, they had made some real progress nonetheless.

"We're not best friends yet," said Ruth, "but we're friendlier than we've been in years."

SIBLING WEEKENDS

One of the most simple but effective means for reconnecting to your siblings or just strengthening sibling ties is a practice called "the sibling weekend." The concept is simple: Siblings get together at an appointed place and time to spend forty-eight to seventy-two hours sharing, recalling childhood memories, having fun, and just catching up and getting to know one another.

The format for a sibling weekend can be totally casual with no particular plan or schedule, or it can include an agenda for discussion. Some siblings may be quite capable of handling intense topics and feelings, but for most people, the best place to start a sibling weekend is by using the same principles outlined earlier: Keep it realistic, reachable, and simple. Following are three examples of sibling weekends that proved to be highly successful.

A Weekend of Childhood Memories. A sibling weekend that included Daisy and her two older brothers lasted forty-eight hours, with most of the time spent just sitting and talking about the old days when they were kids. The order of birth in Daisy's family sounded familiar: one brother six years older and the other eleven years older, almost identical to my own family tree.

"What did you and your brothers talk about during the forty-eight hours?" I asked.

"One thing that struck me was how my older brothers had such different childhood memories of our parents and even our grandparents. Being younger and the baby princess of the family, I had a much different perspective on how Mom and Dad had disciplined us. My brothers let me know they had to toe the line, while I got away with murder."

"Whose idea was it to have a special weekend?"

"My oldest brother brought it up when we were all at our parents' place for Christmas," Daisy recalled. "Up to that point we had had a good relationship, exchanging cards and gifts at Christmas and on birthdays and talking on the phone now and then, but I wouldn't have called us really close. Getting together as we did gave me a lot of new insights on my brothers, not to mention myself. I'm looking forward to doing it on an annual basis."

"Will your husband want to go along next time?"

"Oh no," Daisy laughed. "Before I went on my first sibling weekend he kidded me unmercifully, asking me 'What are you going to do all that time? All three of you haven't been kids for years, so what are you going to talk about?' Then, after I went and had such a good time, he decided that maybe he and his sister should go on a sibling weekend. I told him to do it and to take his mom along, too, and the three of them enjoyed it so much that now they plan to do it on an annual basis!"

A Ladies-Only Weekend. Greta and her three sisters began holding sibling weekends two years ago. The four siblings have continued this practice and will be having their third sibling weekend this year without having their three brothers present.

"We always meet on a weekend, three nights and four days," Greta explained. "We started doing it because we realized our family is so scattered, we've abandoned the family unit and our relationships. Even though I have a wonderful family myself and a lot of friends, I'm realizing that you lose a lot of identity when you depart from your original family. It's been great getting to know my sisters better—in some ways better than when we were kids. We have a wonderful time bringing each other up-to-date on our families."

"Tell me, Greta, on these sibling weekends, have any unresolved issues come up? Have there been any of what you might call confrontations?" I asked.

"Yes, we had that at our first sibling weekend two years ago, and we didn't get it all settled by the time the weekend was over," she answered. "But during the rest of the year through phone calls and letters, some problems got worked out and we were glad to get together again the next year. It seems to me that sisters deal with each other so much differently—I guess that's just the nature of being female."

"Then you've been able to work through some sibling rivalry problems that you and your sisters have had into adulthood?"

"Yes, I suppose you could call it sibling rivalry. While I've been friends with my sisters, it's been more superficial than it should be because we have such different values and beliefs. I'm the only one who goes to church regularly, for example. But as we've gotten older, and particularly because of these sibling weekends, we have more regard and respect for where each of us is coming from. I'm really looking forward to our next sibling weekend. Now when we get back together, we fall right into step with each other. Before, when we were just seeing each other on holidays and such, we felt more like strangers, and by the time we were getting comfortable with each other, everybody had to leave. Now we just pick up where we left off and we're much closer."

"It sounds as if you feel you're a family within a family."

"Oh, yes, definitely. When I got the idea in the first place, I didn't suggest inviting our brothers, and my sisters didn't bring it up either. I'm very fond of my brothers. They have a lot to do with the person I am today, but I felt like I would really enjoy getting together more with my sisters to reclaim our relationship, so to speak."

WHY SIBLING WEEKENDS CAN BE SO VALUABLE

In the two sibling weekends described here you see different combinations and different goals but one central thread: recalling childhood memories. Daisy, Greta, and Zach all felt they had gotten to know their siblings better through hearing them reminisce about their childhood and getting their perspectives on what had happened and how they had been parented.

As siblings recall childhood memories, it is inevitable that they will talk about their parents. For some, memories of parents are pleasant, for the most part, but for others recalling how their parents treated them and their siblings can be frustrating and even painful. Adult siblings who have painful memories of parents may be tempted to turn a sibling weekend into a parent-bashing session. One of the absolute cardinal rules for a sibling weekend should be guarding against letting any particular person lead the group into spending most of the time criticizing parents for their faults and mistakes. As siblings talk, they can acknowledge their parents' mistakes or weaknesses, but they should make every attempt to do this in good humor and then go on to remembering the good times—the memories that will help all of them relate to each other better.

Another significant part of these sibling weekends was the self-revelation, or what Daisy called "gaining personal insights." One of the best ways to grow as an individual is to *So much of who you are today is due to how you interacted together as children many years ago.* spend time with your siblings because so much of who you are today is due to how you interacted together as children many years ago.

Also noteworthy is that all three sets of siblings came together on fairly good terms. While some of the relationships were somewhat superficial, there was not a great deal of anger or a desire to settle old scores. In Greta's case, some tensions did arise, but she and her sisters were able to work through them and build an even stronger relationship.

As you consider having a sibling weekend, don't let possible tension discourage you. Go ahead and arrange the weekend and include a carefully thought-through agenda that makes room for sensitive areas and provides the best approach to covering possible old hurts or even grudges.

A most valuable aspect of sibling weekends is that participants are modeling for their children the importance of having good relationships with brothers and sisters. Anything we can do to curb sibling rivalry among our children will pay off years from now when they become adults and face the problems of relating on an adult level.

Reconnecting

In earlier chapters, I have used the term *sibling moments* to describe times when siblings experience events or encounters that cause strong emotional reaction. Sibling moments should never be confused with sibling weekends, which are normally planned with pleasurable relaxing in mind so siblings can get to know each other better. On the other hand, sibling moments usually just happen—and almost always cause stress and tension.

For example, you will recall Peggy's brothers getting into a fistfight while their mother lay dying of leukemia. And you will also remember Rachel, who at age thirty-one endured a sibling moment when she went home to a family reunion and had her older brothers treat her as if she were a child of ten. This sent her right back into the role of compliant pleaser, something she had been trying to shed ever since getting married to a man who wanted her to be more assertive.

While sibling moments usually involve tension and stress, they don't necessarily have to end in distress or disaster. Even times of crisis and tragedy can turn a sibling moment into a warm reconciliation between brothers or sisters who have been feuding for years.

Esther's Albatross

Such was the case with Esther and her younger brother, Edward. Esther remembers her brother, five years younger, as always being a pest she had to baby-sit or take along with her if she went anywhere with her friends. To be truthful, little Edward was something of an albatross around his sister's neck, and things didn't get a lot better as they got older. Anytime Esther's parents did something for her, Edward wanted equal treatment. As the two of them grew to adulthood, they both helped their parents run the family's mobile-home park.

Eventually they both went to work full time, Esther as office manager and Edward as maintenance-crew chief. Growing up didn't help Edward's babyish desire for all the goodies and kicks he could get, and he became something of a family black sheep. Alcohol was first and dabbling in drugs followed, but

Edward always managed to show up for work and do his job adequately. He was always hard to deal with, however, with a very quick temper. He kept his wife and daughter as well as Esther and their parents "walking on egg shells" to keep him pacified.

Tension kept building for several years like the proverbial Mount Saint Helens. Then Esther's parents asked her and her husband to buy the mobile-home park because they were getting too old for the stress and pressure. Because of his unstable lifestyle, Edward was left out of those negotiations, and when he heard about the new deal, Mount Saint Helens went up with a roar. After the dust had cleared, Edward was out of the family business, and although he lived less than half a mile down the road from Esther, he flatly refused to talk to her despite her repeated efforts to make peace.

This cold war went on for more than five years, and while Edward did speak to his parents off and on, alternately getting along and then getting angry, he never spoke to Esther. Her mother kept saying, "You have to make things right with your brother." Esther's response was, "I want to repair our relationship, but I've gone as far as I feel I can go. I just won't put myself on the line anymore because he always blows up in my face. I'm always the bad guy."

Although Edward and Esther didn't speak, there was one connection between their families. When Edward's daughter, Lori, became a teenager, she started attending the church youth group where Esther was one of the adult leaders. Esther could take Lori to church and she could even telephone her, but only at certain times. Esther had strict orders not to call when Lori might not be there or when Edward might be asleep. On the few occasions when she did call at the wrong time, there were serious repercussions, but somehow Lori was able to stay involved at church.

Three Sibling Moments. Then the first sibling moment came. On a hot summer day Esther became very ill and was rushed to the hospital, where the diagnoses was multiple sclerosis. The second night she was there a nurse told Esther her brother had called and that he would like to talk with her if she wanted to call him back. Esther was incredulous and was sure the nurse was mistaken, but she had Edward's correct name and phone number so she knew that somehow it had to be true.

When she dialed the number, Edward answered. He said Mom had told him that she was sick, and he was sorry about that. In fact, he was sorry about everything that had happened —for the way he had lived and the way he had treated her. He hoped they could start trying to have a relationship again. Esther and Edward both wept on the phone, and in the morning Edward and his wife stopped by with some flowers. They stayed for more than an hour, making small talk. It was a start.

Almost two months later the second sibling moment happened while Esther was still at home, recuperating from her illness. The phone rang and it was Esther's dad, telling her that Lori, her fourteen-year-old niece, had hung herself.

"None of us can get there right now," her dad said over the phone. "Can you go over there and try to help until someone else can come?" No one was home but Esther, and the doctors had warned her to stay away from stressful situations. But she went anyway, and Edward drove up just a few minutes after she got there. They grieved together, and the reconciliation that had begun in the hospital when Esther had been ill became even stronger as tragedy drew them closer to one another.

Esther took care of all the funeral arrangements for Lori, carrying out all of Edward's requests and wishes to the letter. Meanwhile, Esther's church family moved in to help, showering Edward and his wife with food, care, and concern. Edward kept telling Esther, "I don't know how we could have gotten through this without all this wonderful help and love."

Ten days later, a third sibling moment arrived. Edward asked Esther to come over, and when she did he told her his wife had left him. Once again he broke down and shared how sorry he was for how he had acted over the past years toward his wife and daughter as well as toward Esther. Esther simply said that those things were forgotten. And that is what Esther and her brother have tried to do. He has returned to the church and now helps Esther with her youth group work. He speaks often of how overwhelmingly kind everyone was when his daughter died.

LEARNING THE LESSONS

The story of Esther and Edward demonstrates the importance of having realistic expectations in the face of what seems to be a hopeless situation. It often takes a crisis to turn such a situation around, and in Esther and Edward's case three dramatic events happened in the space of a few months to bring about a total change in their relationship and particularly in her brother's life. While few of us may have (or want) such dramatic sibling moments, we can draw several lessons from this story:

1. Persistence and patience pay off. Two keys to saving or renewing any relationship are being persistent and being patient through irritation and discouragement. This is particularly true when a sibling has rebelled against family values. While Esther couldn't quite make the first move toward her brother and it took her serious illness to cause him to act, she persisted in staying in touch with Edward's family and did all she could to be a Christian influence on Lori.

2. Add compassion, kindness, and humility. For years Esther adhered to the strict conditions under which she could maintain contact with Edward's family. Although he never said anything, it was obvious that her kindly and humble approach worked on his hard heart. When she fell ill, that hardness finally cracked. And when Esther and other members of her church showed him deep compassion after his daughter died tragically and his wife left him, his tough shell crumbled completely.

3. Both sides need to forgive. Over the years, Edward had been slowly forgiving Esther, his icy anger melting under her persistent kindness. Then, when he reached out to her when she was gravely ill, Esther was more than ready to forgive him and welcome him back. Obviously, there was no detailed plan or strategy at work here, but simple steps were taken from both sides. Their sibling connection was renewed and became stronger than ever. Forgiveness is a vital part of repairing any relationship. We will look more closely at its importance in Chapter 8.

Forgiveness is a vital part of repairing any relationship.

As you map out your own strategy for reaching out to a distant or estranged sibling, analyze how well you are incorporating the principles discussed in this chapter. Following is a brief quiz to help you assess your strategy.

Assessing Your Relationship-Repair Strategy

1. What do you expect from your adult sibling relationships? Check off any of the following that apply or write in your own answers.

___Friendliness   ___Honesty   ___Vulnerability

___Sharing secrets   ___Loyalty   ___Advice

___A Listening ear   ___Time together   ___Financial sup-
port

___Emotional sup-   ___Better commu-
port   nication

___Other: _____

2. If you have more than one sibling, which one offers the best hope for an improved relationship and why? _____
_____

3. List one to three specific things you can do in the next thirty days to improve your relationship to an adult sibling: _____
_____
_____

Sometimes when you take your first steps to reconnect, the words come naturally, and the lines of communication go back up with relatively few problems. For other siblings, however, it's not quite that easy. The wall of feelings that has formed over the years is not scaled with a single bound. What you may need are a few more tools that can help you communicate your real feelings and desires, specifics on what to say after you get past, "Hi! How have you been lately?"

No set of techniques for communicating is fail-safe. You can always fall flat on your face no matter what you do, but there are ways to approach and confront an estranged sibling to make the odds much better for reestablishing a broken relationship. In Chapter 8 I'll describe some practical techniques I have used successfully with my own siblings to draw us closer together than we've been in years.

Chapter 8

Bridging the Gap between You and Your Siblings

Whether the gap between you and your siblings is narrow or wide, there are three additional steps you can take to bridge the distance. These three steps are essential for anyone who wants to make real progress in improving sibling relationships.

- First, face the truth about yourself and your siblings.
- Second, forgive your sibling, or at least make a start on forgiving and go from there.
- Third, confront your sibling in a caring way, a process called "care-fronting."

Like most steps in a strategy, these three tasks are interrelated. Unless we deal with the lies we've been telling ourselves, we cannot reach out with forgiveness. And if we haven't at least begun the process of forgiveness, how can we confront our sibling in a caring way?

In his fine book, *Caring Enough to Confront,* David Augsburger discusses several principles regarding confrontation that are consistent with my own approach to improving adult sibling relationships. The primary meaning of *confront* that has found its way into our dictionaries speaks of coming face-to-face with someone in a hostile manner. Augsburger observes that the typical approach is to see confronting and caring as almost diametrically opposed actions. We think that the only time we can care is during the tender moments when things are going well or when we're reaching out to console someone. We save confronting for when we're angry and we really want to let people know what we think and how we feel.

Augsburger believes, however, that you can put caring and confronting together and learn how to "care-front" others. To care-front means that you clearly convey your thoughts and feelings, but you do it in a tactful, loving way. He said:

> Caring comes first, confrontation follows. A context of caring can be created when a person is truly *for* another, genuinely concerned about another, authentically related *to* another. The content of such caring is, however, not a blank check approval of the other. The core of true caring is a clear invitation to grow, to become what he or she truly is and can be, to move toward maturity. . . . The crucial element [of care-frontation] is—does it foster growth? Does it invite maturing? Does it set another more free to be?[1]

These lovely words by Augsburger sound great, but for many of us some preliminary work must be done before we can care genuinely and authentically for the sibling who has been distant, indifferent, and possibly even hostile.

Controlling Your Self-Talk

Perhaps the best place to start is with what many counselors and psychologists call our "self-talk"—what we tell ourselves all day long out loud or in our thoughts. Since we can think at the rate of approximately thirteen hundred words a minute, we tell ourselves a lot of things every day. You can't stop your self-talk, but you can control it and turn it from negative to positive.

Dr. William Backus, a clinical psychologist and author, has developed a way of looking at negative self-talk called "misbelief therapy." Backus believes that whatever your feelings are at the moment about someone or some thing, these feelings are not caused by the circumstances themselves but by what you are telling yourself about the circumstances. What you tell yourself is one of two things, the truth or a lie. Backus writes:

> If you tell yourself untruths or lies, you will *believe* untruths and lies. If you tell yourself you are a dumb jerk who can't do anything right, you'll believe it. If you *believe* something, you will act as though you believe it.[2]

Backus goes on to point out that misbeliefs are the direct cause of emotional turmoil, maladapted behavior, and most so-called "mental illness." Misbeliefs also drive people to engage in destructive activities such as overeating, smoking, lying, drunkenness, stealing, and adultery. To this list I would add sibling rivalry.

One obvious misbelief siblings often hold: . . . the siblings, not themselves, are the source of the rivalry!

We've already mentioned one obvious misbelief siblings often hold: they believe the siblings, not themselves, are the source of the rivalry! Another perception that can differ a great deal in siblings is who was the parents' favorite. One sibling grows up sure that his brother was the favorite, while that same brother sees his sibling as the one who got all the breaks. In *Mixed Feelings*, Francine Klagsbrun mentions four sisters who all declared themselves to be their father's favorite, and each one of them was proud to make that claim.[3]

To feel that you're not the chosen one can be a devastating, long-term experience. As an Adlerian counselor, I'm reminded of Alfred Adler's own description of how that feels. He was not his mother's favorite, and because of that, he theorized that whenever a child feels discouraged, the root cause is almost always the feeling that someone else has gained preference or superiority to him. Adler believed that it was impossible for anyone to not become disgusted and irritated if put on a lower level than someone else—and this certainly included siblings.

However wide or narrow the rift between you and your sibling is today, it almost always goes back to your memory of how things were when you were kids. You see it one way, and your sibling sees it another. For example, one sibling recalls being very caring and helpful for a younger sibling; the younger sibling recalls that the older one was bossy and downright abusive at times.

The issue is not whose memories are correct. The point is that it's always important to analyze your feelings about your sibling and challenge what could be lies and misperceptions. At least give your sibling the benefit of the doubt instead of judging him or her. The eye of the beholder may need glasses!

Jesus painted a graphic picture of this when He talked about not judging others because in so doing we only invite judgment on ourselves. Instead of going on indefinitely about how our sibling should change, we can take Jesus' advice in Matthew 7:5: "Hypocrite! First remove the plank from your own eye, and then you will see clearly to remove the speck from your brother's eye."

FORGIVENESS: TAKING A RISK

Before we can confront our siblings in a way that will help heal relationships and not strain them further, we must be sure we have forgiven those siblings. Whatever happened in the past, we need to forgive them for those sins of omission or commission during childhood or perhaps as recently as last Christmas when you both got in a row over nothing.

When Peter came and asked his Master how many times he should forgive, Peter suggested seven times because he knew that was more than double the number of times suggested in the teachings of the rabbis of that day. But Jesus said, "I do not say to you, up to seven times, but up to seventy times seven" (Matt. 18:22). What He was telling Peter was that he should forgive indefinitely.

And if we don't forgive, we are captives in a prison of our own making. Perhaps that's why, in His Sermon on the Mount, Jesus also said that if we forgive others when they sin against us, God will forgive us. If we don't forgive others, we cut ourselves off from God's forgiving grace and the work He needs to do in our lives. (See Matthew 6:14–15.)

In his excellent book, *Forgive and Forget: Healing the Hurts We Don't Deserve*, Lewis Smedes puts it well when he says:

> Forgiveness is God's invention for coming to terms with a world in which, despite their best intentions, people are unfair to each other and hurt each other deeply. He began by forgiving us. And he invites us all to forgive each other.[4]

As I have interviewed and counseled many siblings, they have shared many hurts experienced at the hands of brothers and sisters. They can catalog these hurts in great detail, but what they often fail to see is their need to forgive. Then and only then can healing begin. Such was the case with Brenda and her half-sister Harriet.

INTERFERENCE, RESENTMENT, AND FORGIVENESS

"I guess you could say I have a big problem with only half a sibling," Brenda told me as we talked about her blended family. "My half-sister, Harriet, who is thirteen years older than I am, helped raise my brother and me and I resented how she bossed us around, particularly as I was going through high school. Now that I'm married and have a family of my own, she is still in our lives and wants to be Grandma to my kids. She's not satisfied with being Aunt Harriet—she wants my kids to call her Grandma. She's always bringing them things and wanting to take them places. She's spoils them rotten, and I need to figure out a way to tell her to back off."

"Tell me more about how Harriet raised you and your brother. Where was your mother all this time?"

"Dad had only one child by his first wife, and that was Harriet. They divorced when Harriet was ten, and he remarried my mother two years later. I was born a year after that, when Harriet was thirteen; my younger brother, Dan, was born three years later—that made Harriet sixteen by then. She was always our 'second mom' and had to do a lot of baby-sitting, something she didn't enjoy too much because she had all her teenage interests going."

"That's understandable. First-borns don't always appreciate having to baby-sit siblings—especially half-siblings. Tell me, how did Harriet get along with her stepmother—your mom?"

"Harriet and Mom never got along that well. Harriet married young—at nineteen—and I think Mom was glad to have her out of the house. But when I was nine, Mom got cancer; she died in less than six months. My dad had always been having trouble with alcohol, and this put him over the edge. He tried his best to raise the two of us alone, but he really struggled. My brother especially had a lot of fears and trauma in those years after Mom died."

"What did Harriet do when your stepmother died?"

"By then she had kids of her own, but she wanted to give Dad all the help she could so she tried to mother us as well, something I didn't appreciate, particularly when I became a teenager. But Harriet hung in there and for several years she often took care of my brother and me while my dad was working or getting over another hangover."

"You mentioned that Harriet was bossy. How did the two of you get along?"

"Not all that well. I was pretty rebellious in high school, mostly because of my dad's drinking problems, which made me feel embarrassed and neglected. I got married young too—when I was twenty. My dad died a year later and my younger brother moved in with Harriet and her family for several years while he was finishing up high school and getting through college."

"And so today Harriet is still very involved in your life and Dan's, too?"

"Today I'm thirty-four and have three kids of my own. Dan is thirty-one with two kids and another one on the way. Harriet and her husband live only four miles from Dan and only ten miles from us. She keeps coming over to his house and mine, mostly to see our kids and 'play Grandma.' Dan doesn't mind—in fact, he rather likes it. But I do mind because she's interfering in our family. I call her 'Aunt Harriet' but she tells the kids to call her 'Grandma'; it's very confusing. She's spoiling them too."

"How does she spoil your children?" I asked.

"Mostly by taking them places we can't afford—the newest Disney movie, amusement parks—whatever. Then she's always feeding them junk food. When I tell them 'no junk food,' they say, 'But Grandma Harriet lets us eat it.' "

"It seems to me, Brenda, that the real issue here is control. Harriet was in control most of the time while you were growing up, and you particularly didn't like it when you were a teenager. Now that you're married with a family of your own she's still in your life, and, as you see it, still trying to be in control. This time she's doing it through your kids."

I was tempted to give Brenda some quick lessons in "carefrontation," but I suspected she had some preliminary work to do first. Care-fronting Harriet with some good clear "I-messages" (see pages 123–126), could come later.

I suggested to Brenda that she do some hard thinking about her sensitivity to Harriet's controlling ways because of how she resented Harriet back when she was a teenager. I pointed out that she could well be the victim of her own negative self-talk, which she had been feeding herself all these years as she remembered her own perceptions about the part Harriet played in her childhood.

I also pointed out that perhaps Brenda could be a bit jealous of the fact that Harriet takes her children places she can't afford right now. I let Brenda know that many people would be delighted to have an older and trustworthy member of the family that was interested in their children. I suggested perhaps part of the solution might be asking Harriet to sit while Brenda and her husband have a night out or even a brief vacation. Actually, Brenda could really benefit by having someone like Harriet around. We should all be so lucky!

It's true, of course, that Brenda won't necessarily be able to forgive Harriet in a flash—or even in a few weeks or months. The resentments and hurts that are perceived during childhood become deeply embedded, and it takes time to forgive.

Lewis Smedes points out that for some fortunate people, one

definite decision to forgive is enough. For a lot of us, however, forgiveness is a long journey that starts with being able to at least wish our sibling well.

As Smedes observes, "Forgiving is a miracle . . . that few of us have the magic to perform easily. Never underestimate the demands that forgiving puts on the average person's modest power to love."[5]

TRADING VENGEANCE FOR FORGIVENESS

One of the most well-known and instructive stories regarding sibling jealousy, rivalry, violence, and eventual forgiveness is the biblical account of Joseph and his eleven brothers recorded in Genesis 37. Joseph was the favorite of his father, Jacob, who gave him a beautiful coat of many colors. This was just one of many ways Jacob singled out Joseph as his special son. Because Joseph was only seventeen (and somewhat naive about human nature) he lorded it over his siblings a bit, and this drove them into such an insane and jealous rage that they almost killed him.

Fortunately, Joseph's older brother Judah interceded at the last moment, and instead of killing Joseph they sold him to a passing caravan that packed him off to slavery in far-off Egypt. A most resilient fellow, Joseph rebounded from his mishaps and through a series of personal exploits that would make many of today's TV and film heroes pale by comparison, he rose to become the prime minister of Egypt, second in command to Pharaoh himself.

By now many years had passed, and famine struck in Israel, the home of Joseph's brothers. Because Egypt was known as the breadbasket of the world, Jacob sent his sons to Pharaoh's kingdom to ask if they could buy grain.

The brothers wound up in an audience with Joseph, whom they did not recognize after all those years. But Joseph recognized his siblings. What a sibling moment to indulge himself in revenge! He could literally have had their heads and no one would have even challenged him. But apparently it never even occurred to Joseph to get even. Perhaps he knew instinctively that getting even, as Lewis Smedes puts it, is a "loser's game." But while Joseph had forgiven his brothers, he was not above having a little fun with them—possibly to "teach them a lesson."

Continuing to keep his real identity a secret from his brothers, Joseph put them through some paces—first accusing them of being spies and later of being thieves who had stolen his personal silver drinking cup. When his siblings were totally beside themselves with fear, Joseph finally made himself known to them. Joseph told his brothers they weren't to worry or feel bad about what they had done in the past. He had forgiven them completely and was sure that it had been God's plan to let him be taken to Egypt where eventually he would be in a position to literally save their lives! At this point, all the brothers embraced and kissed each other as they wept with joy.

Why was Joseph able to forgive his brothers after they nearly killed him and sold him into slavery? I believe one answer was in his self-talk. He could have brooded for years over what they had done, then when he finally got his chance he could have had his revenge. Instead, Joseph's self-talk had been positive. He bore his brothers no grudge and forgave them completely.

Granted, it's possible to be a bit cynical about this well-known biblical example of forgiveness. After all, the Old Testament story makes it clear that Joseph had divine help from God time after time after being sold into slavery in Egypt. He could afford to forgive his brothers, because everything had turned out so well.

Similarly, Joseph's story reminds some people of Pope John Paul II, who was shot and almost killed by a would-be assassin early in the 1980s. But the Pope survived and eventually visited the cell of his would-be assassin. The pope took the man's hand and forgave him for his murderous act, a noble gesture. But Lewis Smedes makes the wry observation that "the Pope is a professional forgiver, and it may be easy for such a highly placed professional to forgive when he knows ahead of time that the whole world will be watching. . . . It is ten times harder for an ordinary person, whom nobody is watching, to forgive and forget."[6]

Whenever possible, the process of forgiveness should include coming together with the person you have forgiven. As we look for ways to bridge the gap between ourselves and our siblings, we need to find practical tools that will help us come together in a loving and effective way.

Practicing "Care-Frontation"

Earlier I mentioned David Augsburger's theory about how we can put caring and confronting together and in so doing learn how to care-front others. In other words, we can be open and honest with our siblings, but we can communicate love and caring at the same time.

Care-fronting is an art that can be learned by mastering basic skills of communication.

Care-fronting is an art that can be learned by mastering basic skills of communication such as the following:

1. Focus on behavior, not attitude or character. In other words, become adept at sending an I-message rather than the typical you-message. One of the biggest benefits of sending an I-message is that it forces you to take a hard look at yourself—especially at what you are feeling and thinking at the moment. It is much easier—but much less effective—to send a you-message, which attacks the other person with accusations about attitude or of character.

As children we learn to defend ourselves with you-messages: "You stupid dork" or "You stink." As adults, we become more sophisticated in delivering you-messages, but they are still childish forms of communication: "You don't care" or "You're not fair." To break this cycle, we need to stop, look at ourselves, and analyze our feelings carefully before we speak. For example:

> DON'T SAY: "Must you always be so bossy? You seem to always need to be in control."
>
> INSTEAD TRY: "When I'm pressured to make a quick decision, I start to feel tense and stressed. Please give me a little time to make up my mind."

When I counseled Brenda about Aunt Harriet, she agreed that one of her major problems was a lack of true forgiveness for her much older half-sister. Brenda was willing to try to forgive Harriet, but she still wondered what to do about her rather controlling approach to Brenda's children.

"Take Aunt Harriet out for lunch and talk to her alone," I advised. "Do a little care-frontation. In other words, confront her in a caring way. Tell her just how you feel, but don't attack her character or accuse her of having a bossy or controlling attitude. Use I-messages to explain how uncomfortable you are."

"And what are I-messages?" Brenda wanted to know.

"They are a much better way of expressing yourself than you-messages. Don't tell Harriet, 'You're interfering in our family. You always want to be in control. You're getting the children confused,' and so on. Instead, say such things as, 'I appreciate all the help you gave us when Dan and I were young, but I feel smothered by all the attention you are giving my family. I'm uncomfortable when you ask them to call you Grandma instead of Aunt Harriet. I'm also uncomfortable with the different approaches we have to buying them treats. I really don't want them having a lot of sugary stuff, which I tell them is off-limits.' "

Deciding that I-messages were worth a try, Brenda used them with Harriet the very next time they got together. There was tension at first because Harriet had had no idea she was coming across as controlling and bossy. Eventually, however, they worked out a new arrangement so Harriet could spend time with Brenda's children but only as an aunt who was willing to honor their mother's wishes about going easy on junk food and other things that might possibly be harmful.

2. Describe the situation, but don't make judgments. When you make a judgment on something somebody said or did, you establish your opinion before having all the facts. Inevitably, making judgments closes the door to real communication and understanding.

It is no wonder that Jesus issued dire warnings against making judgments. While the primary meaning of His words in Matthew 7:1, "Judge not, that you be not judged" concerns God's eternal judgment on all men, there is a secondary meaning to be drawn from His wisdom. When you are judgmental, it causes the other person to retaliate by judging you in return. Whenever you attack someone, it is natural for that person to defend himself or herself by going on the counterattack. The only way to break this endless (and stupid) cycle is to describe the situation that you see, but not to make judgments. For example:

DON'T SAY: "Couldn't you have at least called us? It would be nice to get at least that much consideration instead of always wondering when you're going to show up."

INSTEAD TRY: "When you didn't call us, we couldn't figure out what happened to you. I know you would have called if you could have gotten to a phone. I hope everything's OK."

3. Give suggestions or choices rather than advice and answers. This is another excellent way to approach your sibling on an adult-to-adult basis rather than on a child-to-child level or, even worse, an adult-to-child level. Many relationships between friends, spouses, or siblings are marred when one or both parties has all the answers or is constantly giving unsolicited advice. When you give the other person a suggestion or choice, you show that person respect. You let this person know, "I respect your ability to think for yourself." For example, when talking with a sibling about the sensitive subject of how to parent:

DON'T SAY: "I think you should make Jimmy go to bed earlier. Five is too young to stay up until 9:30."

INSTEAD TRY: "Perhaps it would help get Jimmy to bed if you read a story together or maybe played a tape with his favorite music."

4. Be honest and truthful, but don't vent your feelings to put siblings down or "set them straight." In other words, inform and encourage your siblings, but don't give them a piece of your mind. (Have any of us ever really wanted a piece of someone else's mind?) Instead, tell the truth in a respectful, gentle fashion. Your first consideration should always be, "What is in the best interests of my sibling and our relationship?" For example:

DON'T SAY: "I'm tired of competing with you at every level, always feeling that I'm the little kid who has to prove himself and wondering what I'm going to do next to make you jealous."

INSTEAD TRY: "Sometime I feel as if we're in some kind of competition. Do you ever feel that way too?"

5. When dealing with sensitive issues, avoid asking "Why?" and try to focus on "What?" or "How?" "Why?" is an adult-to-child question that forces the other person to give an explanation or an accounting for his or her words or actions. It is a challenge that puts the other person on the defensive.

As David Augsburger says, " 'Why' gets into trying to decipher cause and effect. 'Why' starts with being historical and ends in becoming hysterical."[7] On the other hand, asking "What?" or "How?" is an adult-to-adult question that gives the other person room to breathe and exchange ideas in a more relaxed manner. For example:

DON'T SAY: "Why do you speak to Mom so sharply?"

INSTEAD TRY: "I've noticed you speak to Mom rather sharply lately. What does she do to irritate you? How can we ask her, in a kindly way, to stop doing it?"

If you can master all five of the care-fronting skills outlined here, you are almost guaranteed to be able to improve any relationship you may have. If all five seem too much to tackle at first, start with the I-message, which, I believe, is most important. Then work on the other four skills as opportunities arise. The following story is one example of how to care-front an overbearing sibling.

CONFRONTING THE FAMILY CONTROLLER

In her early thirties, Melissa is third-born in a family of six that includes four sisters and two younger brothers. Melissa lives on the West Coast while the rest of her family, including her parents, all live in a southeastern state. She gets along beautifully with all her siblings except one—her first-born older sister with whom she's always clashed. In fact, everyone in the family has always clashed with Dorothy, who is extremely controlling and critical.

When growing up, Dorothy was always headstrong and hard to deal with, and she and her father, particularly, would always knock heads. Today, Dorothy is a bitter divorcée with two children. To make ends meet she has moved back in with her parents, who both have health problems, including her dad's Hodgkin's disease. Dorothy does her best to care for her parents, accepting little help from the brothers and sisters nearby. Depressed and lonely, Dorothy has decided that all her problems are her parents' fault, and she makes life particularly miserable for her mother with her constant complaints and carping.

When I interviewed Melissa about her sibling relationships, she said she kept in close touch by phone with her other two sisters and her two brothers, and they all got along beautifully. Melissa also tried to talk with Dorothy now and then, but their discussions often turned into confrontations.

"Ever since we were little, I'm the only one who could stand up to her," Melissa explained. "I just don't let her get away with talking to me the way she talks to my mom or my sisters and brothers."

"Give me an example of what Dorothy does that turns everyone off," I asked.

"Well, the whole family can be over at Mom's house—this has happened when I've been back there for Christmas—and we'll all be having a wonderful time when Dorothy walks in. The whole mood changes. She can just ruin a really good time with her way of thinking everything needs to be done a certain way. If it isn't done her way, she becomes very uptight and starts screaming at people—things like that."

"It sounds as if she's definitely the controller of the family."

"Absolutely! I'm fortunate to live so far away that she can't try to control my life, but I wouldn't let her anyway. It's really getting bad for my brothers and sisters though; they keep asking me what they can do about Dorothy."

I pointed out to Melissa that living at a distance from Dorothy and the rest of the family has given her an objective viewpoint that is a strength and an advantage. But I also explained that she was being drawn into a triangle consisting of herself, Dorothy, and the rest of the family. (We'll discuss suggestions for how to deal with sibling triangles in greater detail in Chapter 9.)

"When your sisters and the rest of the family ask you for advice on how to deal with Dorothy, I'd put the ball back in their court as much as I could," I said. "The last thing you want to be is some sort of cop who tries to keep Dorothy in line when she becomes too controlling and belligerent with the rest of the family."

"But that's just the trouble," Melissa replied. "My sisters—and my brothers for that matter—really can't handle Dorothy. They've never been able to confront her, and all their lives she has sort of ruled the family roost, except for me."

"I'm not saying that you can't confront Dorothy on your own over the phone—which I believe you've been doing anyway from time to time," I said. "But I don't think it's a good idea for you to call up Dorothy and tell her that your other siblings have been complaining about her. Keep what you discuss with Dorothy strictly between the two of you and let Dorothy get the message about how she may be affecting the rest of the family. As for your brothers and sisters, one thing they might want to try is to confront Dorothy together, not to gang up on her but to simply give themselves enough mutual support so they can stand up to her and tell her how they feel."

Many of the care-frontation tools we've discussed in this chapter could be used in confronting Dorothy, whether Melissa does it herself or the rest of her siblings try it on their own. Obviously, they want to be honest with her, but they want to avoid venting anger to simply get their feelings "off their chest." In most cases, venting only produces a similar response and, since Dorothy is a controller who is slightly depressed and in a bad mood anyway, you would almost be sure to get more heat than light.

Probably the best tool that Melissa or her other siblings could use would be the I-message, which would focus on what Dorothy does and not on her character or her attitude. The last thing they want to send to Dorothy is a you-message that would tell her, "You're constantly critical, abusive, and obnoxious, especially to Mom and Dad. You're a real wet blanket at any family gathering."

An I-message, on the other hand, could tell Dorothy, "I feel uncomfortable when you come to a family party or any kind of get-together and start telling the others and me what to do . . . I feel bad when you criticize Mom and Dad."

It could also be valuable to describe what happens but not make judgments. It won't help to tell Dorothy, "You were rude and inconsiderate when you switched last weekend's party to a later time without talking to the rest of us to see if that would be convenient." A much better approach would be to simply describe what happened: "When you switched the party to a different time, it really left several of us in a bind with our schedules."

One other obvious observation that I made to help Melissa gain more insight is that Dorothy has been living with her parents and providing for their care. This, in itself, creates a powerful bond between them, and when you add the fact that Dorothy is oldest in the family and feels unusually responsible for the situation, it is no wonder she presumes a certain amount of freedom to exert her control.

"I'm wondering if Dorothy is even aware of how her actions are being viewed by others in the family," I said to Melissa. "And I'm also wondering if some of the other family members couldn't offer to help her with the care of the parents now and then."

"My sisters have offered to help, but Dorothy always tells them never mind, she'll take care of it," Melissa responded.

"That's a typical response from a controller, but I still think they ought to continue to try to be of help," I said. "If necessary, they could insist on certain times just to see if Dorothy might not give in. I think it's important to try to stand in Dorothy's shoes, or as I like to put it, 'get behind her eyes' and see the situation as she sees it. She needs to be in control because she feels she's the only responsible one and she's trying to hold the pieces together. Few passive people would take on the kind of responsibility that she has. For all you know, she may be rather angry about the lack of involvement by the rest of the family, but her controller nature makes her too proud to take any help."

"It sounds to me as if I need to have empathy for Dorothy," Melissa said. "I'll try, but I have to admit it will be difficult."

"Try going back to your early memories, particularly early memories that involve Dorothy. She didn't get the way she is today without some help from her parents and her siblings. It's possible that Dorothy grew up feeling that everybody had to count on her and that she was always the responsible one. As she married and had a family and then went through her divorce, all of this had its effect on making her bitter and critical, but she's still that controller she became way back in those early years."

Before we hung up, I made one more point, telling Melissa, "Siblings almost always think they are innocent of wrong doing; they believe the *other* sibling is always the real problem. This, of course, is seldom the case. It takes two siblings to tangle, and one of the goals of any care-frontation is to see life as the sibling sees it and to understand where you may be part of the problem, instead of putting the entire problem on the sibling's shoulders.

In this chapter I've tried to give you several examples of how care-frontation works, but in the final analysis the only way to find out is to try it yourself. You may be thinking it wouldn't help to care-front your sibling because it will only lead to arguing, a shouting match, or some other kind of Mount Saint Helens scene. It's possible that this could happen, but if you feel the walls are up and the gap between you is growing wider and wider, what do you have to lose?

BRIDGING THE GAP TO MY BROTHER LARRY

When we care-front, it provides an avenue for reestablishing communication lines that are broken or for establishing new lines of communication.

The more I hear about sibling misunderstandings, the clearer it becomes that a primary problem is a simple lack of communication. Here is where care-frontation becomes so valuable. When we care-front, it provides an avenue for reestablishing communication lines that are broken or for establishing new lines of communication based on new understandings. I believe the latter is what happened when I care-fronted my brother Larry.

As I said in an earlier chapter, when Larry came west on a

business trip to make calls in Phoenix and Tucson, he stopped to see me, but the results were anything but gratifying. The familiar equation—Expectations minus reality equals disappointment —was working overtime that week for me as Larry:

- didn't make it to my board meeting when I expected him there.
- paid a hurried visit to my house and seemed preoccupied, when I expected him to relax and spend some meaningful time with us.
- left his motel room (right next door to my office) to catch a plane without a word to me, when I expected him to drop over and say good-bye.

In the days following Larry's departure, I looked back on my week of disappointment, analyzing my thoughts and trying to be as objective as possible about what had happened. I knew that a lot of my sensitivity was attached to feelings I had about how Larry had treated me when we were kids. All the little snubs, discountings, and put-downs were still there, right under the surface, ready to bubble up when any kind of sibling moment occurred.

Well, we had had some sibling moments, three of them in fact; and now it was time that I told myself the truth. Irritating as Larry could be, I was not a totally innocent party—the poor little baby brother who had always been wronged by his older siblings. And Larry was not some kind of unfeeling jerk who didn't even have the consideration to come over and say good-bye. Somewhere in the middle of all of this was the truth.

I decided it was high time for some care-frontation, so I sat down and tried to write Larry an I-message letter, which included the following honest admissions of how I felt:

When you didn't show up for my "Family Life Today" board meeting, I was ticked. When it became obvious that your visit to our house was an obligation, I was ticked again. I was ticked a third time when Cheri made the effort to come to the office to say good-bye while you sat fifty yards away.

As you left town on Monday, I was feeling hurt. Why? As I

analyzed my feelings and thoughts, I realized that it's my problem and not yours. I suppose as the youngest brother, I am still seeking the approval and recognition of both you and Warren. Being the baby of the family does have its problems. It's been mentioned that we have competition between us; I've concluded that competition isn't my issue at all. Instead the important things for me are acceptance and respect.

It has finally dawned on me that what could have been probably will never be. My expectations are unrealistic. In the process of our journey through life, I've set myself up for disappointment. And it's time for me to grow up and smell the coffee. I suppose that part of the process of improving adult sibling relationships is letting go of what isn't and accepting what is.

This letter wasn't written to solve problems or point fingers. It was a simple expression of feelings and thoughts.

Larry, I respect your efforts, commitment, and dedication to work and family. Your talents are many and greatly exceed my own. I'm proud of your accomplishments and proud to be your brother. . . .

I wasn't sure how Larry would reply to my rather extensive I-message, but in a week or two his return letter arrived. He wasn't ticked at all, and in his usual rational style, he explained what had happened. The reason he hadn't come down from Phoenix for my board meeting was that he had a very important luncheon date that day in the Phoenix area with a man he was interviewing for a key position at the Arizona Youth Haven Ranch. The date had been set weeks before and there was no way Larry could have changed it.

When Larry got my message from his secretary, he understood it to say that if he could come to the meeting, fine, and if he couldn't come, that was fine too. He had meant to call to tell me he couldn't come, but he had gotten busy and he said "it slipped my mind."

As for the quick trip to our house, where he had seemed to be fulfilling an obligation, he admitted that he had several things on his mind, including two more appointments to make that day. He was sorry if it appeared that he didn't want to be there.

And, finally, regarding his not saying a personal good-bye, he assumed Cheri had come over to say good-bye for both of them. He was in a hurry to catch a plane, which meant driving clear back to Phoenix, a hundred miles north, and he thought he didn't have time to come over to my office to chat.

COMMUNICATING ON A NEW WAVELENGTH

Larry's letter satisfied me to a certain degree. At least it was a start on communicating on a newer, much clearer wavelength. It was a catalyst that began a valuable process that helped us sort out the insignificant from the important. I found myself analyzing my feelings and challenging my own lies and perceptions. I had expected Larry to do certain things, and when he didn't do them, I got ticked. (E – R = D will get you every time!)

As I challenged my own self-talk, I discovered I was telling myself lies that had formed in my mind during childhood, particularly: To feel valuable I needed my brothers' attention. When I discovered the truth—that I am valuable with or without my brothers' attention—forgiveness was only a step away. As we have begun to communicate at a deeper level, we've worked hard at getting behind each other's eyes and listening to each other with our hearts, not just exhibiting the typical Carlson rationalism. And the more we communicate, the more we feel dammed-up emotions draining away.

I've learned that forgiveness is more than one person saying, "I'm sorry" and the other person saying, "That's OK. I forgive you." Asking for forgiveness and giving it are not just done with words. We behave our way into sibling rivalry, and the process of forgiveness includes behaving our way out of it. For me, forgiveness has intertwined with my own change of attitude, thought, and response to my brother's lifestyle.

Asking for forgiveness and giving it are not just done with words.

And finally, I was able to practice care-frontation at a personal level. I learned firsthand that, instead of making assumptions or jumping to conclusions, *siblings have to talk.* Not long after receiving Larry's letter, I called him on the phone and apologized for jumping to conclusions and getting irritated when I didn't fully understand the situation. He replied that no apology was necessary and, again, he was sorry for the misunderstanding, particularly about the board meeting. That phone conversation led to several others as we continued to explore our feelings and perceptions, not only concerning our adult relationship but also our childhood together. The result is that we're closer than we've ever been and we are relating to each other with a new respect and compassion.

If you're intent on bridging the gap to one of your siblings, use the following quiz to be sure you're ready to take the necessary steps:

Are You Working to Bridge the Gap?

1. What has your self-talk been telling you about your sibling?____

_____

Are you sure you know the entire truth? ___Yes ___No If not, do you think your sibling deserves the benefit of the doubt? Why or why not? _____

_____

2. Have you begun to forgive your sibling for any wrongs he or she has done in the distant or recent past? ___Yes ___No How do you know you have really forgiven your sibling? _____

_____

If you haven't been able to forgive him or her, what's holding you back? _____

_____

3. What behavior or attitude of your sibling would you like to confront? _____
Why? _____

4. What do you believe needs to be changed to make your relationship with your sibling better? _____

_____

5. In what ways have you already tried to confront your sibling? _

   _____

   What has helped and what has not helped? _____

   _____

6. When you care-front your sibling, are you expecting a certain response, or are you willing to let your sibling be free to be who he or she really is? _____

   _____

Before care-fronting a sibling, it might be wise to practice the care-frontation skills described in this chapter by trying them out on people with whom you have a little better relationship, your spouse or a friend, for example. Then, when you're ready, *gently* try care-fronting your sibling. Remember that your goal is not to "set your sibling straight"; if anything, you're trying to set *yourself* straight in order to make things right, because you realize you're part of what's wrong!

In any family, you don't have to look very far to find situations where care-frontation is needed. In particular, family triangles almost always require care-frontation that is done gently, constructively, acceptingly, and clearly. In Chapter 9, we'll see why.

Chapter 9

PUTTING AN END TO DESTRUCTIVE FAMILY TRIANGLES

(The Scene: Mom has just called her daughter, Rose, and she is not too happy because of what she just heard from Rose's older sister, Emily.)

MOM: I've just learned that you charged Emily for the flowers you did for her wedding. After all she's done for you, how can you feel good about letting your sister pay you for things like that?

ROSE: Well, Mom, that was something Emily and I had agreed to. I didn't want to charge her, but she insisted on paying, so I . . .

MOM: Well, I don't think you should have charged your

sister at all. I'm not surprised, I guess, but I am disappointed in you.

ROSE: Mom, this is really none of your business and it really hurts when you and Emily get together behind my back and talk about me. I'm going to call Emily right now— I'm sick of this!

MOM: Well! I don't know why you're so touchy. I was just trying to help. After all, I've always been concerned about you girls getting along with each other.

(Mom hangs up, and Rose dials Emily's number to try to straighten out the misunderstanding.)

ROSE: Hi, Emily. I've just talked to Mom and she seems to think that you're upset because you paid me for doing the flowers for your wedding. As I recall, you offered to pay me, so I don't understand the problem.

EMILY: Well, yes, I did talk to Mom about it. I don't recall that I actually offered to pay you. I thought we were just kidding around. When I got the bill, it about blew me away.

ROSE: You think the bill was too big? I charged you half of what I usually get for doing flowers. If that's the way you feel, why don't we just forget the bill?

EMILY: Now you're accusing me of not wanting to pay my bill! Well, your lousy check is already in the mail! *(Click)*

This brief drama actually happened, and it's a typical example of a family "triangle," one of the key roadblocks to better sibling connections. Triangles are usually caused when Mom (or Dad) gets between two siblings to pass judgment, deliver messages, and cause trouble in general.

Families that are dysfunctional or competitive or play clear favorites, have more problems with triangling. Competition always breeds a win/lose scenario, and whenever a win/lose struggle is going on, participants in that struggle look for an ally, someone to support them in their quest. If they find that someone, they can then take a "we/them" kind of approach, which leads to triangling and destroying of relationships.

In triangling, a family often divides into teams or cliques. One sibling goes to a parent, for example, to talk behind the other sibling's back, and the clique is formed. The dysfunctional aspect of all this is that one sibling feels better about herself if she can get a parent to feel worse about her sibling. It's easy to spot this kind of childishness when you're rearing young children. If big sister can get little brother in trouble, she feels better about herself because she's off the hook and doesn't have to prove herself quite so much. Unfortunately, adults will play the same games but with more sophistication, and that's why it's so easy for triangles to form.

As I talked with Rose, it was not hard to see how her triangle problem had developed. Born third of four sisters, Rose grew up in a home that was verbally and physically abusive, with most of the abuse heaped on her and her baby sister, Marlene. The two older girls, Emily and Vicky, were more the favorites of her parents, whom Rose described as "always being at each other's throats."

She said, "We went through some weird things as kids. I've watched my dad fake a suicide, and for years he packed a .45 automatic all the time. He even slept with it. There were just a lot of bizarre things that I thought were normal—until I got married and had children of my own."

"As all you girls were growing up," I asked, "was it typical for your mom or dad to get between you and cause trouble?"

"Very typical. It's almost as if they seemed to enjoy it. Since this last blowup with Emily, she and I have literally not spoken for over a year. Then all of a sudden out of a clear blue sky I got this envelope with her return address on it, but the only thing inside was an Ann Landers' article that talked about 'reconciliation day.' There was no note or explanation of any kind. When I asked my husband what he thought it meant, all he said was, 'Well, it doesn't say anything to me.' "

Rose went on to explain that because she didn't quite know what the article meant, she didn't call Emily or even drop her a note. Then, a week or two later, she got a letter from Emily that said:

Rose, this is probably the hardest letter I've ever had to write because I don't know what I've done to you to make you totally disown me. When we were younger, we would always have our differences, even knock-down-drag-out fights, but we were always able to forgive each other.

I don't know if it bothers you to not talk to me or see me, but it bothers me. My son is two months old. You've never seen him. I've never seen your daughter, and I hardly know Kurt. Do they even know that I exist?

Do you realize that it has been over a year since we've talked to each other? You are and always will be my sister, and whether you believe it or not, I love you. I don't know what to say to you, but I would like to have my sister back. Life is so short, and I believe we should make every day count. We just never know how long we have with our family.

"So Emily actually took the first step!" I observed with some surprise. "Obviously, she's been feeling bad about your falling out and she's finally decided to reach out to you. She's forgiven you and she's wondering if you can forgive her. Can you?"

"Yes, I think I can," Rose said carefully. "Emily hurt me when she told me off about the flowers and hung up. I've stayed away from her because I thought she didn't want a relationship— and frankly, it's been more peaceful in a way. Anyway, I called her on the phone after I got her letter and we had a good talk."

"Did you talk about the flower incident and get that straightened out?"

"Yes, we talked about it, but I'm not sure we ever got it straight on why I thought she wanted me to send her a bill. We are both willing to let it go. And what really helped was that Emily has admitted that she sometimes teams up with Mom to talk about me and criticize me. She told me she was sorry and that all she wants now is for us to have a closer relationship."

"So what is your next step?"

"We made a date for lunch to talk about it some more, and that's coming up in a couple of days. What I want to know now is, how can I stop my mother from getting so involved in our lives? And where do I go from here with Emily? She seems to want to change, but I'm not sure she can stop running to Mom whenever we have a disagreement."

Learning How to Set Boundaries

"Up until now," I told Rose, "you've been doing what we call *triangling*. In other words, you let your mother step in between you and your sister to pass messages and make judgments. And because of your mother's favoritism toward Emily, it's been easy for the two of them to gang up on you."

"You know," Rose admitted, "it's been that way ever since we were little girls. Whenever Emily and I got into disagreements, Mom would intervene, play judge and jury, and decide what was best for us. I would usually lose."

I explained to Rose that one of the hardest things children have to do, even after reaching adulthood, is to put their parents in perspective. Adult children need to move from the role of the parents' child to more of the role of the parents' friend. This does not mean showing disrespect for parents or refusing to honor them as Scripture clearly teaches. But it does mean that everyone has to eventually grow up and leave home, not only physically, but emotionally. All siblings must learn to stand on their own two feet, and at the same time they need to know when it's perfectly OK to say no to such powerful figures as Mom or Dad.

Becoming an adult doesn't automatically happen by turning eighteen or even twenty-one. Many adults are really little persons living in a big persons' world, feeling what psychologist Henry Cloud calls "one down" in all their important relationships. When you feel one down, you feel that others are above you and your task is to gain their acceptance and approval in order to feel OK about yourself. According to Cloud, becoming an adult "ultimately has to do with coming out from under the one down relationship that a child has to parents and other adults, and coming into an equal standing as an adult on his or her own."[1]

When we set boundaries, we tell others, . . . "This is as far as I go and this is as far as you go."

A major responsibility in being a mature adult is knowing how to set boundaries—for yourself and for others. When you set boundaries, you not only tell people who you are, but you also let them know what you like and what you don't like, what you want and what you don't want.[2] It is important to realize that setting boundaries is not only an act of self-respect, it is an act of respect for others. When we set boundaries, we tell others, such as a parent, "This is as far as I go and this is as far as you go. Within these boundaries we can both operate peacefully and even lovingly together."

But in a highly dysfunctional family, like Rose and Emily's, there were few, if any, boundaries. Mom and Dad saw to that because instead of setting their own boundaries with one another and showing respect for each other within those boundaries, all they did was argue and fight, keeping the family in a constant state of turmoil. With models like this, it is no wonder that their daughters didn't learn how to set boundaries either.

Lack of boundaries was one of the major causes of the mix-up and then the blowup between Rose and Emily. Rose's role in the family was a compliant pleaser, and when Emily came to her for help with her wedding, Rose was more than happy to oblige. She never really wanted to charge for the flower arranging, but when Emily insisted she complied, afraid to offend her first-born sister. When she went ahead and sent a bill, Emily became irritated, and out of habit she told Mom what had happened.

Of course, Mom knew "just how Emily felt," and she also knew exactly "what Rose needed to hear" as well. Mom got into the triangle in earnest by calling Rose and bawling her out. But in a real sense, much of the problem between Rose and Emily was really Rose's responsibility, and I told her as much.

"My responsibility?" Rose shot back. "Emily's the one who got mad at me, swore at me, and hung up. Now she's written to say she's sorry, that she wants to get together, but I'm not very hopeful that anything's really going to change. We'll just have something else come up, my mother will get in the middle, and there will be fighting again."

"The first principle for breaking any triangle is that the shortest distance between two points is a straight line," I explained. "The first thing you need to do when you sit down and have lunch with Emily is to tell her that you're more than happy to forgive but not to forget completely what has been causing your problems. It's not that you want to carry grudges, but you need to explain some specific things that have been happening and how they've impacted your relationship all these years. Both of you need to set some new boundaries with each other and with your mother."

Rose took my advice. When she talked to Emily about keeping their relationship strictly between themselves, her older sister was more than willing to try because she was tired of the triangling too. Then, with a little coaching from me, Rose took Mom to lunch and used plenty of I-messages to let her know that, while she loved her very much, from now on she would prefer that Mom stay out of any situations between herself and any of her sisters.

Naturally enough, Mom was not about to give up a lifetime habit in one lunch. At first she acted hurt, but when Rose would not back down Mom said a bit angrily, "I don't see how you can say all this. I've always just tried to help. After all, I'm your mother!"

But no matter how much Mom huffed and puffed, Rose did not back off. It was hard at first, and Mom continued to make phone calls to let each sister "know how things are." But Rose and Emily had drawn together around mutual boundaries, and they politely but firmly told Mom they weren't interested in what she knew. They told her if there was something to be discussed, they would rather speak directly to each other and not through her. After a few months, Mom got the point and the triangling practically ceased.

HEALTHY AND UNHEALTHY BOUNDARIES

In my advice to Rose, you may have noticed that I suggested that she and her sister set new boundaries and work from there. There had been boundaries of a sort in the past, but they had been unhealthy ones that had involved the mother and one daughter joining in an alliance toward another sibling. Boundaries, in a sense, are "rules of the game." When alliances are part of triangles, somebody gets taken advantage of because the rules are stacked against him or her. Other characteristics of unhealthy boundaries are:

- Inappropriate expressions of anger, bitterness, and resentment.

- Childish behaviors and attitudes, such as cutting off communication, dishonesty, lack of trust, invulnerability.
- Overreliance by one sibling on the acceptance and approval of another sibling or an overconcern about what one sibling thinks or feels.

Healthy boundaries, on the other hand, are seldom part of a triangle. In a family with healthy boundaries, you will see:

- Equality between siblings in their relationships. They may not be the same in their personalities, their likes and dislikes, or even their values, but they are equals as far as adult-to-adult communication is concerned.
- Respect for one another. Siblings respect each other's opinion as well as the opinions of their parents, even though they may disagree at times.
- A willingness to be transparent and vulnerable. Healthy boundaries encourage honesty and the sharing of real feelings. Hidden agendas and facades are stripped away.
- Growth and personal development among siblings as well as the parents.

Before reading further, stop and take the following quiz to analyze possible triangles in your family that may have been caused by unhealthy boundaries.

Analyzing Family Triangles

1. When you and your siblings were children, was the level of competition between you low, medium, or excessive? _____ What part did your parents play as you competed with your siblings? _____

2. How would you characterize your relationship to your siblings today? Check one:
   ___ Win/Lose (Somebody has to come out on top.)
   ___ Win/Win (We work it out so we both feel good about it.)

3. Did your parent(s) talk about your other siblings behind the siblings' backs in ways that created negative feelings? Yes___ No___ Which siblings were talked about? _____ What is your relationship to those siblings today? Good___ Fair___ Poor___

4. As you look back on your family during your growing-up years, what kind of boundaries were there—healthy, unhealthy, or seemingly nonexistent? _____

5. As you look at your relationship to your parents today, have you set any new boundaries with them? If so, describe: _____
_____

6. As you look at your relationships to your siblings today, what healthy boundaries have you set with each other? _____
_____

   Are any of them unhealthy? ___Yes ___No If yes, what are they?
_____

WHEN A PARENT SEES THE LIGHT

In a typical parent-siblings triangle, it is not always a sibling who finally figures it out and tries to break an unhealthy pattern of communication. In one case, Martha, a widow and mother of Joanne and Sherry, came to ask for my help with how to stop serving as a go-between for her two daughters who were constantly at odds with one another.

"Sherry's my youngest and I can see that she's always feeling disrespected and unappreciated by her older sister," Martha explained. "Sherry comes to me for a shoulder to cry on, and I want to be understanding and concerned, so I listen to her. Because I was the youngest sibling in my family, I tend to over-identify sometimes with Sherry, and she interprets this as my approval of her point of view."

"In other words," I interjected, "in her mind, Sherry thinks she has an alliance with you against Joanne?"

"I guess that's one way to put it," Martha agreed. "Sherry will go back to Joanne and say something like, 'I talked to Mom last week and she agrees that you're only interested in your own life and you don't want to spend any time with her now that she's a widow.' Of course, I never said any such thing, so I then have to go back to Joanne and explain what really went on. Then Joanne gives me her side of things, and around and around we go."

"I suggest that you simply resign from this unhealthy triangle," I said. "You can sit down with both of your daughters and talk to them, or perhaps you can write them both a letter; but what you want to say, essentially, is that you can no longer serve as a go-between for the two of them. Tell them that when they have disagreements, you will no longer listen to one sister complain about the other. Say that you will be happy to listen to each daughter talk about her own life and the concerns with her own marriage and children, and you'll be there to help whenever necessary; but tell them you refuse to be drawn into their disagreements any longer.

Martha took my advice, and while it was difficult to confront her daughters, particularly Sherry, it took a tremendous load off her mind. In effect, she broke the triangle by placing the ball back in each daughter's court, where they had to learn to work out their conflicts one-on-one. Joanne and Sherry went through a period of several months of being unsure of how to confront each other, but eventually they developed a much healthier relationship because it was built on mutual respect and healthy boundaries.

In fact, when Martha laid down her rule to no longer listen to each daughter complain about the other, she literally forced healthy boundaries on the two of them. In this way, Martha promoted equality between the two girls and modeled vulnerability and transparency for them as well. As painful as it was, she encouraged them to grow into more mature people.

EMOTIONS EXPOSED WHEN A SIBLING MARRIES

In *Mixed Feelings*, Francine Klagsbrun speaks of the pain marriage causes siblings who have been so close in the past. The special exclusive link they had is broken, and they must learn to relate on a new basis, not only with each other but with the other sibling's spouse.[3]

A sibling's marriage can unearth . . . jealousy or even open hostility between a new spouse and his or her new in-laws.

A sibling's marriage can unearth emotions that can cause jealousy or even open hostility between a new spouse and his or her new in-laws. As one secretary put it, "I was *very* upset when my older brother got married. We used to be so close, and I felt I had lost him to someone who didn't hold a candle to me. I still feel that way. My sister-in-law is no peach!"[4]

Another typical problem is that a sibling who has been reasonable and fairly easy to get along with changes when he or she marries. Old bonds and ties to the other siblings in the family get frayed and sometimes even break because a man or woman decides to leave home and make a separate family of his or her own.

APPEASEMENT OR COMPROMISE?

In Bonnie's case, she had a great relationship with her brother Tom while they were growing up. He was just a little more than two years younger than she, and while they had their fights and disagreements, they were basically very close.

Bonnie recalls an overall good home life in a church-going family. While Tom was always the quieter one, they had a lot of the same friends right up through high school, and they'd go to many church outings, parties, and games together.

Bonnie and Tom remained close well into college. Although they attended separate universities, they stayed in touch because the schools were only two hours apart and they could visit back and forth.

After college Bonnie's and Tom's relationship changed. Bonnie got out of college first, met her husband, and settled down in the Midwest. For the next year or two she didn't see much of Tom, who had taken an engineering job in a western state. Then when she and her husband made a special trip west to visit Tom, he introduced them to Judy, whom he had been dating for several months.

Bonnie and her husband did several things together with Tom and Judy, and everyone seemed to have a good time. Bonnie did notice that Judy seemed seductive and manipulative. It wasn't until several months later when Tom and Judy got married that Bonnie and the rest of the family learned that she was a divorcée and the mother of a three-year-old daughter. Even though they had been in her home during their visit with Tom earlier, Judy had never mentioned her daughter once during the four days they were in town.

"What kind of relationship do you and your husband have with Judy now?" I asked.

"It's not very good. Judy is the baby of her family and she's always gotten just what she wanted. When she doesn't get her own way, she makes people pay. About a year after she and Tom were married we went out to visit them, and we all went hiking together in some mountains that were about a two-hour drive away. On the way back, I suggested we stop to get a quick snack. I didn't know Judy had made something to eat and it was waiting for us back at her house. She didn't say anything, so we stopped and got a hamburger. That made her so angry that the next day she told Tom to tell us she wasn't going to fix any more food, and that we'd just have to go out to eat and pay for our own food. The rest of our visit was pretty uncomfortable and we left sooner than we had planned."

"Judy sure sounds like the baby princess of the family," I observed. "Did anything else happen since that visit to make things better—or worse?"

"Well, actually, worse. About a year later I got pregnant and I called Tom to let him know. Judy answered the phone and I just asked her if they could call back when Tom got home. A couple of hours later he did call back, and I told him about being pregnant, and we had a long talk and finally hung up. Then later that night, he called back—in fact both of them were on the phone—and Judy was very angry because I hadn't been willing to tell her about being pregnant in the first place. Tom accused us of not liking Judy and always leaving her out, and he made it clear that we can tell her anything that we want to tell him," Bonnie said.

"Since that call, he won't take any phone calls at work from us—in fact, he won't give anybody in the family his work number because he doesn't want us saying anything to him without Judy knowing."

"If you could write a letter to Tom that would be for his eyes only, what would you say?"

"Well, for one thing, I'd say that I wish I could see him more often. I'm expecting our third baby, and he's never seen any of my children. I know Tom makes pretty good money as an engineer but Judy spends it rather freely, and they claim they can't afford to make any trips east. I know we can't afford to go out there on my husband's salary as a teacher, so it seems as if we're stuck."

As Bonnie told me her story, it became clear that if she hopes to improve the triangle situation with her brother and her sister-in-law, she will need to take a little different tack. While it is true that Judy is apparently a self-centered baby of the family and that she gets very angry when she doesn't get her own way, it's up to Bonnie to reach out to her sister-in-law with love and respect. As we deal with our siblings and their spouses, it's all too easy to find evidence to justify our own convictions that it's always "their fault, not ours."

Before our interview ended, I suggested to Bonnie that she try to develop a relationship with Judy completely separate from her relationship with her brother, Tom. She could begin by sending her a personal note, a card and a gift on her birthday, or even better, she could call on the phone and talk directly with Judy and not even ask for her brother.

"Those are just some little ways to show that you care for Judy," I said. "At first it may be difficult because it isn't natural and maybe you think you can't even mean what you are saying, but the point is you need to reach out to communicate with her and tell her that she's important to you, just as your brother is. And if you don't mind, I'd like to make one other suggestion."

"What's that?" Bonnie asked.

"If you get pregnant again, please call Judy and tell her *first*. I'm sure Tom won't mind!"

WHEN EVERYONE HAS TO TAKE SIDES

Sometimes in-law triangles also include the parents. Ralph, the number-three son in a family of five boys and a girl, talked to me about a problem that has been going on in his family for more than five years. It seemed that his oldest brother, Jim, first-born in the family, had always been well-liked by his parents—until they had a major difference of opinion, about five years before.

"What kind of difference of opinion?" I queried.

"Jim had been divorced and had remarried. His daughter, Tammy, wasn't getting along with her new stepmother, and Jim decided the best way to discipline her was to kick her out of the house during her senior year of high school. Jim thought Tammy was going to live with a friend, but our parents took her in and he got so irritated at this he broke off communication with the rest of the family. That's the way it's been for some five years now."

"Did Jim think that all of the family was against him?"

"My wife and I tried to stay neutral," Ralph said. "But it turned into a 'you're either on my side or on theirs' kind of thing. It became a real problem for my other brothers and sister and me. Jim was really never that close to any of us."

"How did Jim get along with your mom and dad while he was growing up?"

"He got along great. He was the perfect first-born son and never had any problems in high school. He finished college and worked his way up to regional vice-president in charge of sales for his company. He did everything perfectly—until he got divorced. Then it was as if he rebelled or something."

"So he remarried and his new wife didn't get along with his daughter," I said. "Do you think he put the daughter out of the house to please his new wife?"

"I think that was part of it. Nobody else in the family thought it was right for an eighteen-year-old girl to be out on the street."

As Ralph explained his family situation, I observed that in fact two triangles were probably operating at once. The three points on one triangle (Triangle A, below) consisted of Ralph and his wife, Ralph and Jim's parents, and Jim and his wife. The points on the other triangle (Triangle B) included Ralph and his wife, his brother Jim, and Jim's wife.

Triangle A

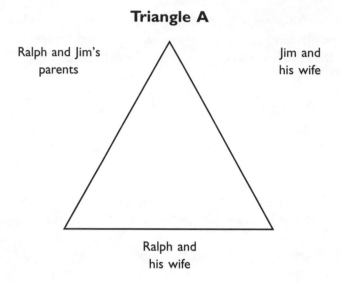

Ralph and Jim's parents

Jim and his wife

Ralph and his wife

Triangle B

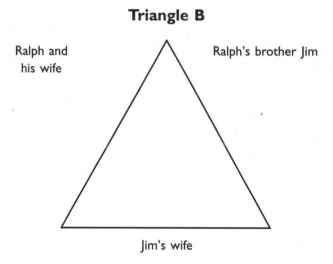

Ralph and his wife

Ralph's brother Jim

Jim's wife

"Let's try to get behind Jim's eyes for a moment," I suggested. "He is suddenly put out of the family and his daughter is taken in. It looks to him as if the family thinks he is the bad guy who has made an irresponsible decision. I'm not judging what your parents did as right or wrong. It does seem to me that if my granddaughter were out on the street, I'd probably open my door too. But the way it all happened caused the family to polarize and take positions. This has been going on for about five years?"

"That's true. His daughter is living on her own now. My parents helped her get through college. Jim totally refused to help with that."

"Do you want to reestablish contact with Jim?"

"Yes. I've talked to my sister and the other brothers individually, and everyone wants to see us get back together as a total family. We invite Jim and his wife to family gatherings, but we never get a response."

"Why don't you try another route?" I suggested. "Instead of sending the usual invitation to a family gathering, just pick up the phone, call Jim, and offer to buy him lunch. It's possible he may turn you down flat, but it's certainly worth a try. My guess is that he wants his brothers and sister to reach out and invite him back in."

"Well, I'm willing to try that," Ralph responded. "But in some ways I think we've got a two-fold problem because Jim's second wife, Rita, perceives that the rest of us didn't make her and her two children very welcome when she married Jim."

"As I said, you can find triangles everywhere, especially when a blended family is involved. But don't let that stop you," I said. "First things first. The principle you should put into action is to keep the ball in the other person's court—in this case, Jim's court. You do that by calling him and taking him to lunch and saying something like, 'You're my brother, and we can't change what's happened in the past, but I want to get back into contact with you. I want to spend time with you. I want our families to spend time together.' That's putting the ball in his court."

"What if he turns me down?"

"Let's face it: It can't get any worse. Go into this with what I call an 'expectations adjustment,' " I suggested. "You're hoping and expecting that somehow or other Jim's going to get back into the family circle, but it could be that his mind is so closed it will never happen. So lower your expectations a bit, and if it doesn't happen, that's OK. The adult thing to do is just confront Jim with love—I call it care-fronting—and let him know where you stand. After that it's his move—and his choice."

"The question I still have about all this is that the problem really seemed to start with his second marriage," said Ralph. "I'm wondering how we can build a bridge to Jim's wife, Rita, who perceives that she isn't totally accepted by our family."

"Why do you think she feels that way? Did somebody have a big wrangle with her when Jim put his daughter out of the house?" I asked.

"No, not that I know of. But over the years my parents have never sent her kids Christmas gifts, for example. My wife and I would try to send a little something, but it was never acknowledged."

"Whenever there's a triangle, it's easy for one party to blame another party for things he or she does or doesn't do," I said. "I think you've done the right thing to try to keep reaching out to Jim and his wife, and I believe you should just step up your program. If you can get Jim to go to lunch and that goes well, maybe you and your wife can invite the two of them out to dinner. But whatever you do, leave Mom and Dad out of it. Don't take responsibility for what Mom and Dad did or didn't do. If Jim brings it up just say, 'Hey, you should talk to Dad or Mom about that. I can't speak for them.' The best way to bust up any triangle is to go the direct route. And when you get rid of the triangle, then you can make progress in your own relationship."

THE IMPACT OF MARRIAGE ON SIBLING BONDS

Like it or not, marriage creates new boundaries between siblings.

In the two case studies described here, we see marriage impacting sibling relationships in a very definite and sometimes destructive way. Triangles often include the sibling's new spouse, but no matter how close siblings have felt in the past, the new marital bond is more important than the sibling bond. Like it or not, marriage creates new boundaries between siblings, and to preserve the marriage those boundaries need to be respected and observed carefully. Use the following quiz to assess how your marriage or the marriage of your sibling has impacted your sibling relationships.

Assessing the Impact of Marriage on Sibling Relationships

1. Has your spouse encouraged or discouraged the bond between you and your siblings? Yes___ No___ In what ways? _____

_____

2. How have you encouraged or discouraged the sibling bond between your spouse and his or her siblings? _____

_____

3. When you relate to your siblings does your spouse say he or she sometimes feels like an outsider? Yes___ No___ If so, describe how this happens: _____

_____

4. As your spouse relates to his or her siblings do you sometimes feel like an outsider? Yes___ No___ If so, describe how this happens: _____

_____

5. What can you do to reduce the tension among siblings on either side of your marriage that has been caused by the marriage? __

_____

While triangling is a major source of tension between sibs, it is by no means the most basic cause. This distinction goes to something we are seldom aware of that controls what we think, say, and do every day—our personal values. In the next chapter, we'll learn why clashing values divide siblings and what can be done about it.

Chapter 10

WHEN SIBLINGS' VALUES CLASH

Dear Randy,
I love my brother and feel as if I've lost one of my best friends. I'm the older one who didn't go to college. We were both saved as teenagers, but Scott "learned better" at the university, where they taught him that religion is nothing more than superstition based on ignorance. Now I can't say or do anything worth listening to. If we do anything together, he calls the shots!

These are the words of a sibling who once had high hopes for his little brother. Unlike so many big brothers, Joel always tried to include Scott in anything he did. When Scott was still too young for Cub Scouts, Joel talked his leader into taking his little brother along on a special field trip that included traveling by train and by bus. Joel remembers, "I couldn't stand the thought of going without Scott!"

But at age thirty-three, Joel is estranged from his twenty-nine-year-old younger brother. He feels he's lost one of his best friends. Why? Because they look at one another today across a wide gulf of different beliefs and values. When I asked, "What would you like to write to your sibling to share your feelings?" Joel put down the following:

Scott, you have accused me of being on a quest to "save" you, but in your eyes you think you've been saved from becoming like me! I wish I could help you see that this is not the case. You aren't like me as far as faith in God goes, that's true; but we still have a lot in common.

I wish I could make you see that God and His teachings are everything to me. God is where my interests are, where my knowledge is, and where my confidence lies. You feel it's perfectly natural for you to talk about any topic relating to your work or areas of interest, but if I say anything that even "smells" of God, you get offended. Scott, I want you to understand that my beliefs are not just some "club" I belong to; my faith is my life—it's me!!!

VALUES: THE GREAT DIVIDE

As I have interviewed and counseled adult siblings, I have found repeatedly that rivalry and estrangement can often be traced right back to personal val-

Rivalry and estrangement can often be traced right back to personal values.

ues—the beliefs, ideas, and attitudes that each sibling feels are most important. By far the most predominant values clash is over differences in faith, a case graphically illustrated by Joel, who writes so poignantly to Scott, almost pleading with his brother to recognize how important his faith is to him.

While differences in faith lead the way, several other value areas also cause a great deal of trouble between siblings. In particular, siblings disagree concerning accomplishments, success, money, and parenting style.

Underlying any values clash is the divisive practice of comparing. Inevitably, comparing puts you into a head-to-head, right-or-wrong, win-lose relationship with someone else. We compare cars, clothes, homes, vacations—you name it. We began comparing when we were children: "Mine is bigger" . . . "She got more ice cream than I did" . . . "I'm stronger" . . . "Who cares? I'm prettier!"

As adults we still compare, but now it's more subtle and sophisticated: "We decided to go with an import—it's so much safer than any American car . . ." "I suppose you can save money at the discount store, but I prefer to shop at the boutique. The quality's so much better . . ."

Comparing puts siblings in an adversarial relationship when they are young, and it continues to do so if they continue the practice as adults. A chief cause of adult sibling rivalry can be traced right back to both siblings looking at one another and seeing differences that cause jealousy, disrespect, and even anger and disdain.

Because values are what we really do—how we really live our lives—and they can be as varied as people themselves. There are, however, several key values areas where siblings often have a clash. Use the following quiz to identify any values areas that may be a cause of division or rivalry between you and your sibling:

Assessing Your Potential for Values Clashes with Your Sibling

Check the values areas listed below where you and your sibling(s) have a clash:

_____ 1. Faith

_____ 2. Money

_____ 3. Parenting style

_____ 4. Work habits

_____ 5. Friendship

_____ 6. Use of time

_____ 7. Entertainment

_____ 8. Family as a priority

_____ 9. Importance of the male role

_____ 10. Importance of the female role

How and why have these values clashes impacted your relationship? Be as specific as possible.

_____

_____

_____

_____

When mounting any campaign to reconcile with a sibling or improve your relationship in any way, it helps to ask yourself some important questions, all of which have to do with personal values—your sibling's and your own.

SAME BACKGROUND, DIFFERENT VALUES

Even if you supposedly were "raised the same way," don't expect your sib to have values that are identical to yours. It is common for one sibling to assume that because his or her parents taught a certain set of values in the home the other siblings also hold those values dear. It is also common to assume that having like values will keep their relationship close even after they leave home.

Whenever siblings do share certain values with equal intensity, it can be a beautiful and inspiring thing, as was the case with Lance and his sister, June. They grew up in a Christian home and became believers at a very young age. On his survey questionnaire, Lance, now thirty-five, wrote to thirty-three-year-old June with this expression of delight in their relationship:

I cannot think of words to describe how grateful to God I am for blessing me with a sister like you. I credit our close relationship to the glory of God. Because of His work in our lives, I can call you not only my sibling but my sister in the Lord as well. It is so exciting for me to watch you grow in the Lord through many of the same situations as myself. I am full of joy to know that we will spend eternity in heaven together still as brother and sister.

Unfortunately, growing up together in the same home doesn't always result in this kind of unity and love. As we discussed in Chapter 4, the paint on your individual portrait dried early as you worked out your lifestyle and life plan. And individual lifestyles don't always match the values taught in one's home while growing up.

For example, suppose two brothers come from a family where the chief value is hard work. The first-born brother interprets this family value as, "If you value work it must come first, ahead of everything else." However, his second-born brother, while a hard worker, refuses to put his job ahead of spending time with his wife and children. The result of these two views of hard work is tension and rivalry between the brothers.

Or suppose you have three siblings who were brought up in a home where the parents were firm disciplinarians. This family value of strict discipline is interpreted in the following individual ways by all three children now that they have families of their own:

- The first-born son, who got the strictest treatment, turns out to be authoritarian and a strong believer in spanking his children with a paddle for any infraction of the rules.
- The second-born in the family, also a boy, believes in running a tight ship, but stops short of spanking except in extreme cases.
- The third-born in the family, a girl, interprets discipline as teaching children responsibility for their actions by making them face logical consequences when they break family rules. She has never spanked any of her children.

When all three of their families come together for picnics, reunions, or Christmas, for example, they experience plenty of tension and friction over their differing approaches to the same general value system all three of them grew up with: firm discipline in the home.

SIBLINGS IN A FAMILY BUSINESS

Clashing values, birth order, and triangles were all involved when I counseled members of a family business that had begun with a grandfather, been passed on to his son, and now included the son's four adult children. Although their father had never made it officially clear, first-born Bob is presumed to be the one who is being groomed to take over the car dealership. Marge, the first-born girl in the family, is on a career track as she heads up the accounting department. Third-born Susan works in inventory, but only on a part-time basis. The baby of the family, Jeff, heads up the service department.

In counseling the four siblings, I dealt with them individually at first to get their uninhibited input on how each saw the situation.

Bob only seemed to have two problems: one, the lack of specifics on the part of his dad and grandfather concerning the direction of the business and plans for his future succession, and two, his sister Marge.

"She has always tried hard to compete with me, even when we were small," Bob recalled. "Now that Marge has earned an accounting degree, she thinks she's qualified to be chief financial officer of our dealership. I keep telling her and the rest of the family she should stay home with her kids."

"How do you get along with your other siblings—Susan and Jeff?" I asked.

"Susan's OK. At least she's not on any kind of career track. Her job in the inventory department is strictly part-time and she'd rather be home with her kids. I really think a woman's place is in the home, if at all possible, but I realize she needs to make some money to supplement her husband's income. As for Jeff, he's a godsend because I don't understand the service end of the business at all. Jeff's always right there, eager to get the job done."

Not surprisingly, when I talked to Marge I got a much different picture.

"Bob is just like Dad," Marge said with a trace of bitterness in her voice. "He's dictatorial, he won't listen, and things have to be done his way. He never takes my ideas seriously. He treats me much like my dad has always treated women—with a lack of respect. He really wants a man in my position, but I'm doing a great job and everybody knows it."

"What was it like when you two were kids?" I asked, feeling fairly certain about the answer.

"You know, it's funny," Marge said after a few seconds, "but

I can remember as kids it was just the same. Bob and Jeff would never let Susan and me play in ball games with their friends, even though we were pretty good. They'd always tell us, 'This game is for boys only, so get out of here and go play with your dolls.' I guess that's how they feel about us today—they want us to stay home and play with our dolls."

Susan concurred that she didn't see her involvement in the car dealership as a long-term career. As for Bob and Marge not getting along, Susan just shrugged and said, "They've never gotten along ever since I can remember. Bob was always trying to let everyone know he was the oldest, and Marge was always showing him up, particularly by getting good grades in school. In this case, though, I'm all for Marge. She's a wiz at accounting, and Bob is just being pigheaded by not listening to her more."

Jeff, the baby of the family, made it clear he wanted to stay detached from the wrangling, but he made some of the most insightful observations of all. "Bob has always felt pressure from our dad to perform and become the future president of the dealership," Jeff commented. "Dad's problem is that he never spells anything out or makes it clear what his plans are. Marge is always on Bob's case and challenges a lot of his decisions, and when Bob tries to ignore her, she just goes directly to Dad and tells him where she thinks Bob is off base. Then Dad has to get involved in the decision making, even though the responsibility of operating the dealership day-to-day belongs to Bob."

"Do you think Marge would really like to run the dealership herself?" I asked Jeff.

"I don't think so," he replied. "It's just that Marge really wants recognition for who she is and what she can do. But she puts Bob in a bad spot when she goes straight to Dad and makes Bob justify what he's doing and why. It keeps the tension at a really high pitch, and it's affecting all of our families. We seldom get together anymore for holidays or cookouts or anything like we used to."

Armed with the information I had gained from my separate interviews with the four siblings, I contacted their father and asked him for some time alone. Mr. Johnson was glad to comply because he, too, was feeling the tension; things were not going as he had hoped.

He was well aware that Bob and Marge were not getting

along—he agreed that they never had, even as children. What he had failed to see was that he had to step in, take authority, and straighten out the issues that were not clear, particularly his plans for Bob to take over the presidency of the company. Also, he needed to spell out a much clearer job description for Marge and just how much authority she really had. She needed to understand that she couldn't go around Bob to come to him when she didn't agree with what Bob was doing.

Mr. Johnson listened carefully as I made my analysis. Finally he said, "I suppose you're right. Confronting people and spelling things out has never been my strong suit—I was always better at selling and making deals. But I guess I had better do something because we can't go on the way we have been."

I assured Mr. Johnson that I would be glad to facilitate some initial family meetings where these matters could be spelled out in detail. I admitted that it would not be easy and there might be some tension and possibly even some angry exchanges, but something had to be done if the business was going to continue to prosper. As he and I worked together on some basic procedures, I learned that there were no policy manuals and there never had been any kind of formal staff meetings or board meetings of any kind. It took several initial sessions involving Mr. Johnson, Marge, and Bob to get things straightened out. Then we brought in the other members of the family to get everyone on the same wavelength concerning what was going on.

All these meetings were the beginning of a family council that met regularly to discuss how the dealership was going. Specialists who advise family businesses say that the composition of the family council can be limited to only family members who are active in the business, but unless there are strong reasons to the contrary, the family council works most effectively when all family members and their spouses are part of the proceedings.[1]

"Look," I told Mr. Johnson and Bob one day at lunch, "all family members have a stake in the dealership, directly or indirectly, and spouses will find out what's going on anyway. They might as well find out firsthand and get the story straight to begin with. That's why I'd include everyone in your family council."

Bob and his dad agreed, and that's how their family council started and how it functions today. The spouses of all four Johnson siblings have been openly appreciative of the new council arrangement, because in the past they never quite understood what was going on and it caused tension between them and other in-laws.

One of the most obvious values areas that had to be dealt with was Bob's attitude toward Marge—and women in general. It turned out that Marge was very correct in saying that Bob had learned a lack of respect of women from his father. Mr. Johnson's value system (which he had learned from *his* father) held that men run the family and they are the ones who are in charge. While he admired Marge's abilities and wanted to give her a chance in the company, the bottom line was that he didn't plan on having her be president. That position was to fall to Bob.

Fortunately, Marge accepted this decision, and in fact, once Mr. Johnson made his plan clear, everyone seemed to relax. As time went by, Marge quit going around Bob to complain to her father, and Bob learned to accept Marge as a capable member of the team. He even began soliciting her advice from time to time. In a few months, the Johnson car dealership was on a much better keel, and Dad was able to slip completely out of the business and let Bob take over with Marge as his key financial officer.

WILL THEY EVER CHANGE?

While the story of the four siblings who worked for their father in a car dealership came out with a happy ending, nobody's basic values changed that much. Bob remained a chauvinist at heart, and Marge was still an aggressive advocate for women's rights. But they did learn to respect and accept each other's values, and that is the key to why they are getting along, not only as business partners, but as siblings.

Whenever one sibling expects another sibling's values to change, . . . that almost always means trouble.

Whenever one sibling expects another sibling's values to change, he or she is putting conditions on the relationship, and that almost always means trouble. As angry as I was with my brother Larry when I wrote him that letter asking why he didn't say good-bye, I believe I was already beginning to realize that I couldn't expect Larry to change all that much. He will always be a very busy guy who may or may not find it necessary to be as socially sensitive as I think he should be. If I keep expecting Larry to change, I'm only putting unnecessary demands on our relationship.

It would be easy enough to fall into the same trap that entangles many siblings when they become offended by a brother or sister—declaring a cold war and just not speaking for months and even years. In *Adult Sibling Rivalry,* Jane Greer tells of how a brother refused to talk to his sister for six years after she turned him down when he asked if he could borrow her luggage for a trip he wanted to take. After repeated urgings by his wife, the brother decided to call his sister to see if he could patch things up. He sent her an I-message, letting her know his feelings had been hurt by her turn-down, but he wondered if they couldn't sort things out.

To his dismay, his sister didn't warmly accept the idea of getting together, nor could she even seem to remember the incident—at least she acted as if she couldn't remember. She told him she would give this some thought and get back to him. She never did. Now the brother was tempted to be angry all over again, but instead he decided that continuing the cold war wasn't worth it. His sister was his sister—no more and no less— so why have unrealistic expectations? By putting aside his anger, the brother "has moved beyond the cold war—he has thawed out of the deep chill the conflict cast over him—and he can now focus more energy on his relationships with his wife, his children, and his friends."[2]

Many values aren't necessarily wrong; they're just different. The point is, neither Larry nor Warren is going to wake up one day and start to think just as I do. Nor am I likely to change as much as they would like. As I counsel adult siblings who are having problems, I see repeatedly that their expectations are not only unrealistic, but unwise. They are expecting a sibling to change. They never say anything like, "If only I could change and become more accepting." It's always, "If only my brother or sister would change, everything would be OK."

THE CASE OF THE BLACK-SHEEP BROTHER

On the other hand, some siblings have to deal with a brother or sister whose values are so diverse from theirs that they have little hope of working out a good relationship. That seemed to be the case with Lucy. As she explained her relationship with her black-sheep brother Earl, it not only appeared hopeless, but it was obvious there was abuse involved as well.

When I talked with Lucy, I could see that one of her problems was that she kept expecting Earl to change, but when she pressured him, it only caused him to become angry and abusive.

"When my mom married my dad, everyone told her she was 'too young,'" Lucy told me as the story of her family unfolded. "But even more important, she had been raised a Christian and my dad was anything but. He was wild and drank too much, but she was crazy in love with him. Her parents tried to tell her she was making a big mistake, but she wouldn't listen."

"What are your early memories of what life was like with your mom and dad?" I wondered.

"My mom tells me that when I was born, my dad seemed to settle down for a while, and he cut way back on his drinking. Then my brother, Earl, was born three years later and for some reason Dad never liked Earl. I can remember Dad always telling Earl that he was no good, that he would never amount to much, that he should straighten up, and all that kind of thing. When I was ten and Earl was seven, my dad started drinking again as well as running around on my mother. Finally, he left us cold and Mom filed for divorce. During divorce proceedings, Dad even blamed Earl for that. I know that doesn't make any sense, but it all just continued to confirm the black-sheep role Dad had laid on Earl, even when he was very young."

"How did you and Earl get along growing up together?" I wondered.

"We fought a lot. After I became a Christian in junior high, we definitely went in different directions. Mom started going to church a lot more faithfully after the divorce, and I went with her. But Earl did everything he could to skip church. Sometimes he would sneak out of Sunday school and Mom wouldn't even know. By the time he was in high school, Earl was drinking a lot and hanging out with a bunch of guys who loved to ride motor-cycles."

The rest of Lucy's story was predictable. Earl moved out by the time he was eighteen and continued a life of drinking, drugs, and running with his biker buddies. By his late twenties, he had a severe drug-abuse problem, and when he agreed to go to a Christian rehab center for alcoholism and drug addiction, Lucy and her mother were thrilled. Their hopes were dashed, however, when Earl dropped out of the program after complet-ing only half of it.

Less than a year later their mom died of breast cancer, and now Earl refuses Lucy's repeated attempts to contact him, say-ing he wants no more to do with the family because he "can never be good enough anyway," he says.

"One of the things we know about children is that they tend to live up to their parents' expectations," I pointed out to Lucy. "When your brother got assigned the role of black sheep by your dad, he had to live that role out because in a twisted kind of way, he wanted to please his father in the hope that he would like him better. To not play the role of black sheep was too risky for Earl, and now that he's an adult the role is just too comfort-ably familiar to change. What he's really saying is that he doesn't think he could be good enough to be the kind of person you are. He'd rather go on playing the black sheep."

Besides the drinking and drugs, another major bone of con-tention between Earl and Lucy was his live-in relationships with different women. When she invited him to spend Christmas with her family (the first Christmas following the death of their mother), Earl asked her what she thought of his current live-in partner. Lucy told him that it was wrong. "You've been through a Christian rehab center," she reminded him. "You know very well what you're doing is wrong."

When Earl started swearing at her over the phone Lucy be-came very frightened because her brother could be very violent; he had physically hurt her when they were younger. She man-aged to interrupt her brother's screaming and swearing and tried to calm him down. "Listen," she said, "I just called to invite you for Christmas because this was our first Christmas without Mom and I didn't want you to have to spend it alone."

"Well, I don't have the money to get there, and I'm not coming," snapped Earl, and he hung up.

"I'm sorry I make Earl so angry," Lucy said as she recounted the incident. "I try not to judge him, but when he asks my opinion about his lifestyle, I have to tell him the truth."

I tried to explain to Lucy that whenever Earl called to ask her opinions on his lifestyle, he already knew the answer. All he was doing was holding up a mirror to remind himself once more that he was the "bad guy" of the family. Instead of giving Earl the answer he wanted, I suggested to Lucy that she could reply by telling Earl the more important question is what he thought of his new relationship with a girl—what did he think of how he was living?

Lucy observed that Earl would probably tell her he thought his lifestyle was perfectly OK and I agreed that would probably be the case, but the important thing was to always throw the ball back into Earl's court. Lucy had to do all she could to keep from reinforcing the black-sheep role Earl had always had. In a sense, Earl was trying to pull her into a triangle relationship with him and his new girlfriend. By refusing to pass judgment on his lifestyle, she could stay out of the triangle trap.

Lucy and Earl were a graphic example of how values are a compass that gives each person a sense of direction in life. A problem for many siblings is that their compasses are pointing in different directions. Lucy, for example, was headed due north and Earl due south! As sibs continue in the direction their values take them, they may feel they increasingly have little in common. It is easy to emphasize differences and fail to see similarities. The truth is, however, that all sibs have much in common if their different values haven't pulled them too far apart.

One obvious thing that siblings have in common is the same genetics. They sprang from the same parents, the same homes, the same family atmosphere. If sibs can recognize the importance of these common ties, they may be able to bridge their differences and values.

Avoiding Clashes in the Valley of Values

In many cases, it is a good idea to stay away from "the valley of values." For example, if you clash with a sibling over how he or she disciplines children, avoid that subject if at all possible. If you clash with a brother who has a materialistic lifestyle and spends too much money on cars or health clubs or whatever, steer clear of that area when you're together.

It is a good idea to stay away from the "valley of values."

Steering clear of controversial areas is not compromising; it only makes good sense if you want a relationship with your siblings. Your siblings are valuable for who they are, not what they believe. I am sometimes misunderstood when I make that statement during counseling or in seminars, but I mean it sincerely. The values your sibling holds are very personal and they took a long time to become a part of him or her. You will not change those values by arguing or criticizing. If anything might cause your sibling to change, even a little bit, it will be through loving and accepting that sibling for who he or she is.

The Center of the Triangle

I interviewed one sibling who seemed to know instinctively that he needed to steer clear of the valley of values. He and his sisters had widely diverse value systems, and while he hoped for change, he knew that any changes that might occur would have to come over a considerable amount of time. Ironically, however, he himself was an exception to the usual rule that values seldom change quickly. His values had changed radically when he found a completely new outlook on life through faith in Christ. For Gus, the old had passed away and the new had come.

When Gus became a Christian at the age of thirty-nine he decided it was time to mend some fences with his family, particularly with his older sister, Amy, whom he hadn't seen for almost six years. He got her phone number from his grandmother, but several attempts to call her ended in frustration. She and her husband never seemed to be home and the messages he left went unanswered.

Then a sibling moment intervened. Gus's grandfather died, and he got to see Amy at the funeral. While his parents and younger sister, Diana, were cold and detached, Amy was open and friendly. She apologized about not answering his messages —they had just replaced their answering machine, she said, because it had been malfunctioning. As Amy and Gus talked, they were able to sort out why he hadn't called her and why she hadn't called him for all those years. It seems that it had revolved around their parents, who had been very disapproving of Gus's lifestyle when he was younger. Strict religious legalists who ran a very tight ship in their home, the parents were extremely authoritarian, especially the mother, a domineering woman who ruled the roost.

While Diana, the youngest sibling, had gone along with her parents' rigid value system, both Amy and Gus rejected their legalistic brand of religion. Amy did her rebelling quietly, going along with her parents to keep the peace. But as soon as she could she moved out and married a man who was nominally religious, at best.

Gus, on the other hand, was particularly wide open in his rebellion, getting into alcohol, drugs, and having several live-in girlfriends before getting married. While Gus and Amy had been quite close while growing up, his radical, rebellious lifestyle drove a wedge between them. After reaching adulthood they had gone their separate ways, staying in touch through their parents. Whatever Amy heard about Gus from Mom and Dad was usually negative. All this negativity only served to separate Gus even further from Amy and his parents. The more negative a triangle situation is, the greater the distance there will be between the three points, in this case, Gus, Amy, and their parents.

Opening Up Old Relationships. When Gus finally divorced his wife at the age of thirty-two, his parents felt it was the final straw. They vowed to have nothing more to do with Gus and they tried to convince Amy she should do the same. Deep down, however, Amy was still fond of her brother and every now and then she would try to rescue Gus from his wild and woolly ways. But she was always rebuffed, and finally she gave up in disgust and despair. Her husband tried to console her, saying, "Look, it's not your fault Gus lives the way he does. He'll never change, so why keep beating your head against the wall?"

And that's how the situation remained, right up until Gus's remarriage, spiritual conversion, and initially unsuccessful efforts to tell his family that he was a different person. Attending Grandpa's funeral was the sibling moment Gus needed to "open up the old doors" with his sister.

"Amy was skeptical about my religious experience," Gus said, "but she still told me that if I could ever come up to her house, they had plenty of room. Well, after the first of the year we did get together and I brought my kids with me for a weekend. Amy's kids were real receptive to my kids, whom they had never met. It was like one big, happy reunion, and Amy just cried and cried with joy. Then, just the other day I got a phone call from her. It was the second time she's called since we visited, and it's just great how we're doing together."

"Have you ever thought about all those years you and Amy lost when you didn't speak?" I asked.

"I sure have. When you lose something like that, you want to try to get it back, and fortunately, it happened. I realize now how important family is, and I don't want to lose my connection to Amy again."

"Why do you think you grew apart?" I asked. "Do you think it was your parents?"

"Yes, a lot of it had to be my parents. They still aren't speaking to me, by the way, even though I've told them I've become a Christian. When I rebelled against all their rules and regulations, they pretty well disowned me, and now it really hurts because they don't seem able to forgive. I wish I could make them realize that what I have is for real. I'm not conning them the way I used to."

"So your new faith has been a real turning point for you?"

"Absolutely. And Amy and her husband, who are nominal church-goers, have noticed. He was in a social-action kind of church when they got married and she has sort of gone along with him. But when we got together that weekend, my brother-in-law told me he had never seen anybody change so much for the better in his life. 'So whatever you're doing, it's great,' he told me."

Closing the Gap with Closer Values

It's important to note that when Gus found his new faith and a whole new set of values, it actually closed the distance between him and his family and made it easier to bridge the gap to his older sister, Amy. While her religious views are not the same as his, they are much closer than they used to be.

As for breaking through to the rest of the family, Gus has a long way to go, but he may succeed as long as he maintains his present attitude of acceptance and forgiveness. His parents and his younger sister may not be quite so ready to do that, and he may face more suspicion and rejection. If he becomes disillusioned or even judgmental because the rest of his family "won't forgive even though they say they're Christians," he will be doomed to disappointment.

Gus shouldn't expect his younger sister's values to change appreciably. Diana will probably always have the same legalistic approach to life that her parents do, and if Gus fails to understand that, he is simply setting himself up for failure. The formula proves out every time: Expectations minus reality equals disappointment.

If Gus will simply try to relate to Diana without expecting her rigid view of the Christian faith to change that much, he stands a much better chance of improving relationships. It does little good for one sibling to judge another for being too rigid and unloving. Rifts of unforgiveness have become canyons of estrangement and even hatred because both sides refuse to take the first step, but as Gus saw, one first step can lead to another, and sibling bonds that have been broken for years can be reforged.

Values Improve with Age

The case studies in this chapter have demonstrated in different ways how values clashes cause rivalry and division among siblings. As you seek possible parallels to your own situation, remember:

Never underestimate the power of values.

Personal values differ greatly from the lists of character traits that we are taught as children (truth, justice, honesty, integrity, responsibility, etc.). Personal values are not just what we are supposed to believe; personal values are what we really believe because they are reflected in what we actually do, how we live our lives from day to day.

Second, although I have explained that you shouldn't stay up nights expecting your siblings' values to change significantly over the short run, it is also true that values can and do change over the years. Significant life changes, which might involve spiritual conversion, a radical change in health and physical condition, loss of business or financial status, and the death of loved ones are some of the forces that can alter your views of what is important at the deepest personal level. I have seen it happen in my oldest brother, Warren, as well as in Larry and myself.

A few months ago Warren and his wife, Barbara, visited us in Tucson and we all went hiking on a scenic trail in the nearby Catalina Mountains. As Warren trudged along ahead of me, I saw a mirror image of myself eleven years from now—same height, same build, even the same facial characteristics. It occurred to me that although our lives had taken different paths we still had a great deal in common, especially the strong personal commitment to family and career development. Hard work, loyalty, and a sense of responsibility were just a few of the values we shared.

Warren had poured his life into his family and his business. He and Barbara had reared three daughters who were now grown, married, and raising families of their own. He hadn't had a lot of time for his brothers over the years (the Carlson "too-busy syndrome"), but now that was changing. Warren had made a special effort to make the trip to Tucson from his home in Muskegon, and he had been particularly warm and friendly the entire time. Although well past the parenting duties Donna and I were facing, Warren had joined with Barbara in listening with interest and empathy as we shared some of the newest challenges offered by Evan, our budding teenager; Andrea, our preadolescent who sometimes thinks she is already an adult;

and D.J., our precocious baby of the family who was currently exploring the mysteries of third grade.

Several months after Warren's visit, I began work in earnest on this book and decided to set up a telephone call to Warren in Muskegon while Larry was visiting him. That day the Carlson brothers spent an hour and a half on the phone, sharing insights, feelings, hopes, and dreams. How we had been brought up, our relationship to our parents, our relationships to each other, our different values, and where we see our lives going today were all topics of conversation.

As we talked, Warren confirmed what I had seen on the Catalina Mountain trail that day. His values had changed over the years as the stress of career had taken its toll.

"As I've gotten older and the nest has emptied, I've begun to look back at my roots a lot more," Warren commented. "I always wanted to get together more often with you two, but never seemed to have the time. Now I'm looking forward to doing it regularly."

I asked Larry if he felt the same way, and he responded, "Yeah, I do. Twenty-five years of doing a lot of the same stuff gets a little old. All of a sudden what really counts is your family relationships."

"You know," Warren interjected, "there is another thing that has hit me hard recently. I look around and see guys who are retiring at fifty-eight or sixty-two or sixty-five. A lot of men aren't retiring later, but earlier. And I see myself at fifty-one, seven years away from some who are retiring right now. And I think, Here I am, fifty-one—and the average life span is seventy. That means I've got nineteen years left on this earth, and when you look at how the last nineteen years passed so quickly, I realize that nineteen more is just a drop in the bucket."

"So you see Larry and me and Mom and Dad, as more important right now?" I asked.

"Definitely," he said. "It was more important to spend time with Mother and Dad this summer than it's ever been before. It's really true—the family becomes more important to you as you get older. When you're a teenager and even in your twenties and thirties, you don't put too much stock in your original family. You're too busy doing your own thing. But as you get older, the importance of where you came from starts to hit you hard."

After our call ended, I sat for a long time, thinking of how our three lives had been drawn closer together as we had shared across two thousand miles of phone lines. I had arranged this call with mixed motives. Yes, of course, I had hoped to gather some grist for my writing mill, but far beyond that I had secretly longed to draw closer to my two brothers, who had always placed me in the role of the family baby, "little Fat Butt" who was always a likely target for teasing.

Perhaps I had always valued our sibling bond more than they did simply because it had always been more important to me. Our phone conversation seemed to humanize our relationship and create a setting for new levels of vulnerability between us. I think we all came away realizing how important the sibling bond really is.

I also came away with a new answer for why it's important to make the effort to build meaningful sibling connections. As Jane Leder says, "The answer is *Whatever our differences, the basic value of the call of kin would always hold us together.* simple: the call of kin. Our basic need to belong to and be part of family demands that we at least try to rest old antagonisms and move on to higher ground."[4] Whatever our differences, the basic value of the call of kin would always hold us together.

Chapter 11

WHAT TO DO IF YOU HIT A "BLANK WALL"

Gail came from a big family with three older brothers, two younger brothers, and her older sister and herself in between. As Gail put it, "I never had any trouble with the boys, but my sister and I never bonded even though we were closest in age and shared a room. She was two years older and that made her two years smarter in everything—at least, that's what she liked to tell me all the time we were growing up."

"Did either of your parents favor any of you?" I asked.

"Well, now that you mention it, if they favored anyone, it was Margie. Mom had three boys in a row fairly close together, then they waited almost four years before Margie was born. By the time I was born, Margie had been the baby princess of the family for a while and she didn't want to give up that role, I guess. She was always bigger, and prettier, and smarter. In fact, when we were young, I just wanted to be like her, but she never gave me a break. She would always put me down and call me "stupid," and stuff like that. When we got into high school, she had a lot more dates than I did, which she never let me forget. We were never friends."

"One reason why your parents may have favored Margie is that she was the first-born girl after having three boys," I suggested. "I suppose your folks had about given up on ever getting a girl, and when Margie came she was special. She sensed that special treatment and never wanted to give you a chance to dethrone her."

"Oh, I don't know what she was so worried about," Gail said almost bitterly. "She had all the looks, all the brains, and a lot more friends. It was like I wasn't there a lot of the time. And it's like that today. I'd like to have a sister, but she just doesn't seem interested. When I have to call someone, I call one of my older brothers. When I do talk with Margie, it's as if she's not there with me. She's somewhere else thinking about more important things. There is just no connection and sometimes I wonder if I should give up. Do you think there is a chance I could ever have a relationship with her?"

The good news for Gail is that she has brothers with whom she bonded, and her relationship to them is stable and nurturing. The bad news is that her relationship to her big sister, Margie, is in "blank-wall territory"—there's "nothing there" and the relationship is going nowhere fast. Gail's failure to feel a genuine connection to Margie is unfortunate but not unusual or rare. Siblings who don't bond are far more common than most people might guess.

If you feel you might be in blank-wall territory, the following quiz has been designed to help you sort out your feelings and decide where to go next. Check the statements that apply to you:

____ 1. I feel discouraged whenever I think about my sibling relationship.

____ 2. I can't think of one thing I've tried that has helped our sibling relationship.

____ 3. I feel as if I'm the only one trying to improve our sibling relationship.

____ 4. I can't trust what my sibling tells me. He or she says one thing and does another.

____ 5. I feel like giving up at working at a relationship with my sibling.

If you've checked only one or two of the above questions, it may be time to try a new approach to your cold or distant sibling rather than continuing to have repeated efforts hit a blank wall. The following case studies contain some practical suggestions for building a new plan of action rather than remaining at the foot of the blank wall, feeling irritated or angry.

OVERCOMING THE "IF I JUST TRY HARDER" SYNDROME

So often a sibling who feels totally shut off by another sibling will think it is "my fault." Adults who hit a blank wall with one or more siblings in their family are often compliant pleasers, so it's typical for them to think that whatever is wrong, they must be to blame. If they can "just work hard enough," maybe they can improve their relationship.

That was the case with Lucy, the older sister whose story was shared in Chapter 10. She kept trying to rescue her black-sheep biker brother, Earl, but because she was a committed Christian, Lucy could not approve of Earl's wild and immoral lifestyle, particularly his string of live-in girlfriends. Yet she felt guilty; she believed if she could only be loving enough he might "come around."

You probably recall that I advised Lucy to keep the ball in Earl's court. I suggested that the next time he called and asked what she thought of his new girlfriend Lucy should avoid answering directly but simply ask him what he thought of how he was living.

A few weeks after our first conversation, Lucy called me back and said, "I've tried doing what you suggested. Earl called me just last night and he already had another new girlfriend. When he asked me what I thought, I 'put the ball back in his court' as you said, and asked him what he thought of it. He just laughed and said he thought it was fine."

"Did you try apologizing to him for the things you said about his lifestyle in the past?" I asked.

"Yes, I did, but all Earl did was talk about how self-righteous Christians are and how they're always putting people down. He never did seem to accept my apology."

"So you've tried to put the ball back in his court, but he doesn't seem to want to play. Is that it?" I said.

"Right. He seems determined to live his own kind of life and he just wants to call me now and then to bait me and have a little fun. He still likes to tell me that his biker friends care more about him than I do," Lucy replied.

"It sounds as if you've pretty well hit a blank wall with Earl," I observed.

"You mean I should just write Earl off and never talk to him again?" Gail wondered.

"No, not at all," I assured her. "I don't believe any sibling is ever totally hopeless and should be abandoned completely. But at the same time you need to face reality and be willing to grieve your losses. The values gap between the two of you is just too wide, at least right now. For the time being, at least, you should give up trying to have any kind of good relationship with Earl. It may be hard, but it's the healthiest thing you can do—for both of you."

GRIEVING YOUR LOSSES

Giving up a relationship with a spouse, a lifelong friend, or a business partner can be difficult, even devastating, but giving up the possibility of having a good relationship with a sibling can sometimes be worse because there is not the same opportunity for closure. After the tragedy of divorce, there is an ex-spouse. If a job is lost, there is an ex-boss. But when we lose a relationship with a sibling, we can't make a clean break because there is no such thing as an ex-sibling. That sibling will always be our sibling, and we still have a responsibility to love our brother or sister as best we can.

There is no such thing as an ex-sibling.

"Giving up on a sibling" doesn't mean you cast your sibling out with dramatic statements such as, "I don't have a brother

Give yourself permission to grieve your lost sibling, and then move on with your life.

(or a sister) anymore!" Instead, you *give up the expectations* that you've had in the past. You reset your goals and realize that your sibling is simply not interested in having a better relationship with you—at least right now. If you keep hanging on to unrealistic expectations you can become frustrated, bitter, and possibly depressed. You need to make a clean break with those kinds of expectations, give yourself permission to grieve your lost sibling, and then move on with your life.

One of the best ways to make this break involves writing a letter to your sibling that you never mail. In this letter you can express all the anger and frustration you feel regarding the loss of the relationship and the lack of a real connection. Pour it all out on paper and then put the letter away for safekeeping. You can take it out and read it again in a few months, or possibly in a year or so, to see if you've made any progress on the frustration and anger you may feel now.

One approach to giving up on a sibling that I do *not* recommend is having a direct confrontation; this usually closes the door permanently. In Lucy's case, I suggested that she sit down and write a letter to Earl, pouring out her heart about how she feels about his lifestyle and how she wishes they could have a better relationship as brother and sister.

"You won't mail this letter to Earl," I reminded her, "but it can do a lot to help you work through some of your frustration, anger, and grief."

"I'll try doing that," Lucy agreed, "but what happens the next time Earl calls to bait me and give me a bad time?"

"The next time Earl calls be friendly, but be firm. Don't let him draw you into arguments or scream and swear at you. Tell him that you care about him and you always will, and whenever he's willing to talk on a civil basis, you're available."

Another idea I gave Lucy was writing Earl the kind of letter that she *would* mail. This letter would contain plenty of I-messages telling him kindly but firmly: "I really feel our current relationship isn't healthy for either of us . . . I love you and want to help you but sometimes I feel my very sanity is threatened. I don't want to be asked what I think of your lifestyle. If you don't want to change, I will love you anyway but I can't stand the continual arguing."

I cautioned Lucy that in writing this kind of letter she should not give any final ultimatums, but at the same time she should firmly tell Earl how she feels. Then the next step is up to him and he has the opportunity to act in a more mature fashion.

Waiting for a Miracle

An important part of grieving your losses is adjusting or lowering your expectations to almost zero. From now on, you will expect nothing from your estranged sibling in response to any communication or concern you express. If you do get back some kind of response, that is a serendipity for which you will be glad, but you won't leap to the conclusion that now your sibling is going to want a warm relationship.

It usually takes a sibling moment of significant proportion to really change things. Sometimes it's a death, an illness, or an accident. With Esther and Edward, the siblings we discussed in Chapter 7, it took three horrific sibling moments to bring them back together: Esther's serious illness, the suicide of Edward's daughter, and the subsequent desertion of Edward by his wife.

In other cases, however, a sibling's life can change in miraculous ways, as we saw with Gus, the black-sheep brother described in Chapter 10, who finally reconnected with his estranged sister, Amy. His conversion experience literally changed many of his values, and he began wanting to have a close relationship with his siblings and even his judgmental, angry parents.

Another important function in the grieving process includes giving yourself permission to be angry about your loss. Just as gasoline moves a car, anger is the fuel that moves us in a positive or negative direction. Anger can be a constructive force to right a wrong or straighten out a warped and unhealthy situation. Or anger can be a destructive means of showing we're not in control. The point is that our anger produces certain thoughts that then create certain reactions. It's not true that people go "blind with anger" and aren't able to think. They are thinking, all right, and they can choose to think in a constructive or destructive way.

When discussing how to handle anger, I often use the simple equation E + T = R. E is the event that causes us disappointment, frustration, pain, and eventually feelings of anger. T is the thought that follows the event, and R is our reaction, which is shown through our behavior.

Suppose, for example, you have tension with a certain sibling and that sibling does something to cause you disappointment, frustration, and eventually anger. As you think about this event in the next few seconds, minutes, or hours you can decide how you will deal with anger. Be aware that being angry is not necessarily wrong or unhealthy; how you handle the anger is the issue.

The most common unhealthy way to deal with anger is "venting" or *expressing* your anger in an out-of-control fashion. In other words, you "lose it." But an even more unhealthy approach is *repressing* your anger—denying that it even exists and refusing to admit, even to yourself, that you are angry. Repression of anger is often a problem for my Christian clients who have been taught that anger is always bad and that no good Christian would ever be angry.

Better approaches to anger include *suppression* and *confession*. When you suppress your anger, you "count to ten" and make a sincere effort to control yourself. This is helpful, but it really doesn't help you get to the root cause of your anger. Confession of anger is also a positive way to handle angry feelings, as long as you admit your anger to the other person in a respectful and controlled way. One of the best tools for doing this is the I-message, described in the section on care-frontation in Chapter 8.[1]

But confession is not the total answer either. While confessing or suppressing anger is a far better approach than venting or repression, no approach to anger will totally deal with the problem until you are ready to admit to yourself *what you are really angry about*. You must go below the details, the often petty stuff that has seemed to cause your anger, to dig down and find the real reason you feel upset.

When confronting a blank-wall situation, it is best to deal with angry feelings alone. Don't try to explain them to your sibling; this will usually only end up in misunderstanding or an all-out battle. Sit in a quiet spot or go for a walk, perhaps, and think it through. Instead of saying, "I am angry because my sibling never calls," or "I am angry because my sibling always takes advantage of me," get to the root of the problem. Admit to yourself, "I am angry because my sibling doesn't respect me," or "My sibling acts as if I'm not there," or "My sibling makes me feel guilty."

Even then you are not finished. Next you must tell yourself the truth about these angry feelings and how you will allow them to affect your life. If you admit, "I'm angry because my sibling does not respect me," and then tell yourself the lie, "Therefore I feel worthless and unlovable," you will remain defeated (along with continuing to feel angry). If you prefer the truth, however, you will tell yourself, "Yes, I am angry because my sibling doesn't respect me, but that doesn't make me undeserving of respect. I am still a worthy person, and while I don't like my sibling's attitude, I can accept it and live with it."

All of this simply means you must change your self-talk when dealing with anger. Telling yourself lies with your self-talk (your thoughts) is a certain way to wind up trapped in the Cain and Abel syndrome. As you tell yourself self-deprecating lies about why your sibling makes you angry, you only feed your anger and your feelings of pride, jealousy, stubbornness, condemnation, and reproach.

Telling yourself lies with your self-talk . . . is a certain way to wind up trapped in the Cain and Abel syndrome.

As I worked with Lucy, she admitted that hitting the blank wall with Earl left her feeling angry because he always made her feel guilty, or as she put it, "like I'm not a good person." As she changed her self-talk about Earl, Lucy was able to work through her anger. She learned to tell herself, "I am not responsible for Earl or what he does. I can love Earl, but for the time being I will have to let him go."

As you work through your anger concerning a blank-wall sibling, it helps to come up with a term or phrase you can use to describe that sibling. As we pointed out, you can't really call this brother or sister an "ex-sibling." In Lucy's case, she could call Earl her "prodigal brother," which would imply that she is still waiting for him to come home. In Gail's case, she could call Margie her "distant sister." The term you choose to use is not important as long as you don't make it one that sounds derogatory or hateful. One thing you should never do is permit yourself to hate your siblings. Dislike their lifestyle or off-the-wall values, but always seek to love them as best you can.

AVOIDING THE VALLEY OF VALUES

A blank-wall situation with a different twist occurred with Bruce and Phil, two brothers who had gone into a construction business together. When I met them, they had been building custom homes on speculation for about five years with Bruce, the oldest, working on the financial side to handle property procurement, bank loans, and such. Phil, two and a half years younger, ran the construction end, supervising the on-site operations.

For the first few years, all had gone well as both siblings seemed to share the same vision for getting their business off the ground. Of late, however, tensions had arisen in their business relationship that were spilling over into family life at home. Both wives were involved in the stress, and in fact it was Sally, Bruce's wife, who suggested that the two of them come to see me, "just to get things sorted out."

As both men told me their story, they seemed to be relaxed and in a good humor, but it quickly became apparent that they had individual value systems that weren't meshing all that well. When counseling siblings who are in business together, I often find relationships that have hit a blank wall even though both parties seem to be getting along quite well. On the surface all looks serene, but just underneath there is a clashing of priorities and goals that is leading inevitably toward real trouble.

If you are a sibling who is in business with another sibling, you may be in the same situation. By suppressing or even repressing your anger, you are keeping the lid on in an effort to get along in a day-to-day working relationship. But in the long run, you and your sibling business partner are going down different paths, and an explosion is almost inevitable. Some of the issues that were taking Phil and Bruce in different directions included:

- Phil wanted to spend more dollars on equipment and tools, while Bruce wanted to get by with what they had.
- Bruce wanted to expand into construction of commercial buildings while Phil wanted to solidify and hold tight to their current firm position in the custom-home field.
- Phil wanted better compensation for his skilled people, particularly lead carpenters, while Bruce wanted to freeze all salaries.
- Bruce wanted to bring his wife, Sally, into the business while Phil felt the wives should remain out of the business completely.

I told the brothers it sounded as if they had some serious differences, and I asked them how they had gotten along while growing up. How had they settled their differences then? I asked.

"Our parents were very firm on the two of us not fighting or arguing," Bruce said. "They often stepped in and settled our problems for us."

"That's a pretty accurate picture," Phil agreed. "We were taught to get along, and anger was always a big no-no."

"What I'm hearing is that the two of you grew up learning to be polite, but to bury your feelings and not be confrontational when any problems arise. And now that you're in business together, you don't really feel like confronting one another, so you just let the problems ride, hoping they will solve themselves. Even worse, you take the problems home and vent your feelings there with your wives. Do I seem to have the correct picture?"

Both men looked at each other sheepishly and nodded. "What the two of you need to do is sit down and develop a strategy or plan for your company. I've listed your four major disagreements here on a sheet of paper, and I think all of them are solvable if both of you are willing to compromise and work toward what is best for the company."

Phil's short laugh revealed his frustration. "That's just the trouble," he said. "We both think what we want is best for the company. We're 180 degrees apart on several things."

"One thing you both need to understand is that you have different values," I pointed out. "I know you think you have the same value system—working hard and doing a good job to make the best product possible. That's all true, but individually you're very different. Bruce, you hit me as a risk-taker, but at the same time you're a little bit tightfisted. Phil, what you value could be called 'doing the job.' You like working with good tools and top-notch equipment, and you want your men to be paid well. At the same time, as the second-born in the family, you've become something of the pleaser, trying to go along with Bruce because he's always been older and the leader."

Both men smiled and admitted that I had them pegged quite well, but they wanted to know, "Where do we go from here?"

In the next twenty minutes, I helped Phil and Bruce develop a problem-solving strategy that included consulting a financial adviser they both trusted to work out their basic issues. A major objective was working out some kind of "missions statement" that would reveal if they both had the same vision for the company that they held when they had started it. Another major assignment was to work through the issue of whether wives should be involved in the company or not. When sibling business partners are in disagreement, bringing a spouse into the picture almost always increases the friction.

When Bruce and Phil sat down with a business adviser to sort out their problems, they learned that their individual values were too strong to be brought together with compromise. Bruce definitely wanted to branch out and go beyond "just building a few nice homes"; he had much bigger goals in mind. But Phil simply wasn't interested in pursuing them. And the other disagreement on which neither man would budge was bringing Sally into the business. Bruce knew she could give invaluable help, particularly in the financial area where he was falling behind with bookkeeping chores. Phil, however, stood pat: "No wives involved in the company."

The bottom line was that both men hit a blank wall as far as their business was concerned. Fortunately, they still had a great deal of affection and respect for one another and, with the help of their consultant, they worked out an amiable parting, with Phil selling out to Bruce and going to work for another contractor of custom homes in the city. This took all the pressure off Phil, who had always been somewhat uncomfortable with the role of business partner.

Bruce went ahead and hired Sally and she was able to straighten out a lot of the bookkeeping snarls by working only on a part-time basis. With Phil's help, Bruce was able to find another construction supervisor who was willing to work on his terms, and he did go into commercial construction with some success. In this unusual case, two siblings lost a business partnership, but they kept their personal relationship intact, and the two couples grew even closer after the brothers dissolved their partnership. Their story is a good example of how avoiding the "valley of values" can save or improve a sibling relationship.

FUTURE EFFECTS OF LACK OF BONDING

A key reason why Bruce and Phil were able to work out their business problems amicably and preserve their personal relationship is that they had bonded as siblings when they were younger. Despite all their differences, they truly liked and loved each other. When siblings don't bond during childhood, they are much more likely to hit a blank wall as adults. This appears to be what happened to Peggy Say, sister of Terry Anderson, the Associated Press journalist who achieved the unenviable distinction of becoming the American hostage held longest by Arab terrorists.

When Anderson stepped out of a helicopter to freedom on December 4, 1991, his sister, who had worked unceasingly for his release for more than six years, hugged him fiercely, believing that from that day on they would have a close relationship. But she was mistaken. What she had forgotten was that she and her brother had never been close as children. Their parents had both struggled with alcoholism, and Peggy, the second oldest of six children, had coped by trying to run away from home several times. Terry, a quiet, studious loner who was seven years younger than Peggy, tried to escape his dysfunctional home life by burying himself in his books. As Peggy summed it up, "None of us were ever close; survival was an individual struggle."[2]

Terry seemed friendly enough the day he and his sister were reunited, but then he was whisked away into a whirlwind of press conferences, television appearances, and numerous ceremonies to honor his homecoming. Several days later, Terry and

Peggy were together for a brief, ten-minute photo session, and it was then he told her he had to get away to be with his fiancée and their six-year-old daughter, who had waited faithfully for him throughout his captivity. Wondering when her brother would ever have time for her, Peggy told him she'd be glad to see him when he got back.

But Terry never really got back—at least in the sense of getting back in touch with his sister who had labored so long to gain his release. She had pleaded with presidents, prayed with spiritual leaders, and confronted politicians and diplomats in Washington, D.C., and the Middle East. As part of preparations for Terry's homecoming, she and her husband had bought a cottage next door to their home in Cadiz, Kentucky, on the shores of a beautiful lake. It was to be a gift to Terry, but he never responded to his sister's repeated attempts to have a close relationship.

In her article, "The Dream That Died," which appeared in *Redbook* magazine, Peggy Say wrote openly about what happened and how heartbroken she was by her brother's lack of interest in her and the rest of the family. Although she did not use the term, Peggy realized she had hit a blank wall as she wrote:

> Inside I cried. Part of me realized that Terry and I had never been close, that he had always set his own agenda without paying too much attention to me. . . .
>
> But the plain truth was, Terry has never given me much of himself or his time. His career was his life, then and now. I'd orchestrated a fantasy that he couldn't possibly have lived up to, indeed, after his return, Terry *needed* to focus on himself, to summon every ounce of energy he had left just to exist.[3]

Peggy realized her brother had to adjust to a new family (he and his fiancée were planning to marry) and the overwhelming problems of being a celebrity who was hounded at every turn by people who wanted interviews, appearances, and the like. She knew Terry was well aware of what she had done for him, but she suspected that perhaps he simply couldn't cope with that—there was too big an emotional debt that he could never repay.

Over the months, however, Peggy, and her husband, David, worked through their grief about the brother and brother-in-law who would probably never be close to them. And Peggy did keep in touch with Terry with occasional phone calls and visits. Their relationship improved, but while he was friendly, conversations remained at the surface level. By then, however, Peggy could handle it. She appeared to have worked through the grief of her blank-wall situation when she said, "I'm not sure if Terry will ever discuss our past problems, or say the words, *Thank you*. I've learned not to expect too much—it's time we both got on with the future."[4]

The Root of Many Bitter Rivalries

Another frequent cause of the blank wall is money. Financial circumstances can put siblings so much at odds that animosity, hostility, and greed make the situation hopeless. And it's not unusual for a triangle to be part of the problem too. That was the case with Maxine, first-born in a family of five, who included two more sisters born second and third and two brothers born fourth and fifth.

Their parents had divorced when Maxine was in high school and Brett, the youngest brother, was only four. Maxine's mother had remained a single mom. Not surprisingly, she had favored Brett, her youngest, who got away with murder while he was growing up. After Brett graduated from high school, he continued living at home and paying no room and board as he attended junior college classes off and on and dabbled in one minimum-wage job after the other, not sticking too long with anything.

Maxine's mother had been the "glue" that kept the rest of the family together. She had also been the apex of any number of triangles because she always let everyone know what was going on with their siblings. As Maxine put it, "She would let us know exactly what was going on in each other's families and her opinion on every situation."

In his mid-twenties, Brett was still living with his mother when she died after contracting breast cancer. Because she was the oldest child in the family, Maxine was made executor of the estate. Now the tension that she had always felt with Brett came to a head. After the funeral expenses and clearing up the remaining mortgage on their mother's house, there was no money left to keep supporting Brett in the manner to which he had become accustomed.

"Brett sees me particularly as the cause of all his problems because now he's had to grow up and start supporting himself," Maxine related.

"How do you get along with your other siblings?" I asked.

"I get along fine with my other sisters and older brother. But when I try to reach out to Brett, he just shuts me out and finds some way to really hurt me. And now that I've had to shut off his support money, he won't even talk to me," she said.

"There is a point, Maxine, where you simply have to grieve your losses, establish some new ground rules, and then move on," I told her. "You might want to drop Brett a note and let him know you had no choice in shutting off his support because there was no money left in the estate to continue supporting him. Then you'll just have to wait him out."

Other points that applied to Maxine's situation were:

- While the death of the mother was tragic, it did have one positive effect in knocking out a major side of all the family triangles she had created between herself and her children. Now that Mom was gone, there was a wonderful opportunity for all of the siblings to develop new ground rules in their relationships.
- No sibling is responsible for the kind of relationship her parents had with another sibling. In other words, Brett may have lived off his mother while she was alive, but now Maxine is not responsible for what went on between Brett and his mother.
- If at all possible, it is imperative that parents have a will that reveals all of their desires openly before they die. In this way, there are no surprises or arguments when the estate is settled. In her will, Maxine's mother had designated Maxine executor of the estate but had not spelled out completely the distribution of some of her personal

possessions. This left Maxine with the unhappy task of deciding who got what and, while some of the items were "little things," it is usually the little things that cause the big problems.

- In many cases, it is advisable to get a non-family member involved as executor of the estate. This is especially true if there is any tension or jealousy between siblings (the heirs). While an eldest son or daughter may be able to do the job, in situations such as Maxine's, tension and even hostility can arise. In cases like this, where a sibling's income has to be cut off, it's always better to get an outsider involved in the role of playing the "bad guy."

- Finally, Maxine needed to be reminded frequently that she was not "mom number two" of the family. She needed to resist telling herself the lie that somehow she was overly responsible for how everyone felt.

LOVING YOUR "BELOVED ENEMY"

Maxine faces a problem I have seen often. Because of parental favoritism and comparisons when they were children and the subsequent disagreements over money, a sibling has practically become an enemy. Maxine doesn't want to be enemies with the sibling who is estranged from her, but she seems trapped at the base of a high and thick blank wall. At this point Jesus' teachings about loving our enemies becomes very personal, particularly His words in Matthew 5:46: "If you love [only] those who love you, what reward have you? Do not even the tax collectors do the same?"

Maxine isn't alone. In a sense, every sibling who throws up a blank wall and won't let you through is your "beloved enemy." The challenge is to love this enemy who will always be a

Every sibling who throws up a blank wall and won't let you through is your "beloved enemy."

part of you without feeling hatred, anger, or guilt yourself. It is no easy line to walk, as many siblings can tell you. But if you're willing to make the effort, there are things you can do. The following list suggests some steps you can take in your strategy for "where to go from here." Check the things you will be willing to try:

_____ 1. I will send cards at Christmas, birthdays, and anniversaries.

_____ 2. I will write an occasional note just to stay in touch, even if I receive no replies.

_____ 3. I will make occasional phone calls to try to talk with my sibling.

_____ 4. I will attempt to communicate through another sibling, spouse, or someone else who has a better relationship with my "beloved enemy."

_____ 5. I will pray frequently for my sibling and our relationship.

_____ 6. I will try to set up a "care-frontation" with my sibling to reestablish communication.

PLAYING THE WAITING GAME

Mapping out your strategy for dealing with a sibling's blank wall doesn't mean you are writing off that sibling forever. Your blank wall may only last six months or a year. On the other hand, it may last for ten years or more. Remember, the Berlin Wall was supposedly impregnable, destined to stand forever, but it eventually came down! Your blank wall can come down too.

If you believe in the power of prayer, keep turning your estranged sibling over to God. Patience, persistence, and unconditional love will go a long way toward bringing the blank wall down some day.

There is no need to make a formal announcement to your estranged sibling that you feel you've hit a blank wall. Try to keep some kind of communication going even though you receive very little in return. The concept of the blank wall is for your own benefit—actually, your own sanity. By realizing that you've hit a blank wall of some kind, you are able to develop a strategy that will make living with this problem easier—and healthier.

Be ready for those sibling moments that will inevitably come to possibly tear the wall down. It may be a death, a tragedy, a crisis—these things always come to every family. In these moments, anything can happen. Old grudges can dissolve, and anger and hatred can melt away as siblings know the freeing power of forgiveness.

In the meantime, the blank wall is there and one way to deal with it is to strengthen your support base by nurturing any positive relationships you have with other siblings in your family. Beyond that, there is one other very practical goal for you to pursue: to raise your own children in a way that keeps them from being entrapped in strong sibling rivalry.

While some families produce siblings who are incredibly good friends (for example, the Mandrell sisters, the Wright brothers, Kathryn Hepburn and her siblings), the much more common situation is that children engage in rivalry to one degree or another. As they compete for power or status in the family, they complain, criticize, and even come to blows. Every week we receive many calls from despairing parents who want to know what they can do to stop all this fighting and bickering among their kids. In Part 3, we'll look at what to avoid, as well as what you can do to reduce sibling rivalry among your children.

Part 3

REARING SIBLINGS WITH LESS RIVALRY

(and less hassle)

Chapter 12

Avoiding the Mistakes That Create Sibling Rivals

When I talk about adult sibling rivalry at a seminar, I'm often asked, "How can I raise my own children so they won't be such rivals? It's starting to drive me nuts." And then the harried parent usually goes on to describe a typical day in the sibling-rivalry pit, a place of screams, shouts, cries of pain, and accusations such as,

- "You did it on purpose!"
- "Mom, he's hitting me!"
- "She got more than I did!"
- "He's been in my room AGAIN!"

From thousands of conversations with parents, I believe it's safe to say that more siblings are rivals than not. Why? I think it boils down to two reasons:

1. Siblings become rivals naturally, with no help from anyone. The scarcity mentality ensures that. Most child-rearing specialists agree that at the root of the scarcity mentality is a child's deep craving for the exclusive love of his or her parents. And with the arrival of each additional sibling, the scarcity mentality increases because it means there is less time and energy for each child. As a result, siblings perceive that there is also less encouragement, less admiration—less love. Adele Faber and Elaine Mazlish, authors of *Siblings without Rivalry*, observe:

> No wonder children struggle so fiercely to be first and best. No wonder they mobilize all their energy to have more or most. Or better still, ALL. Security lies in having all of Mommy, all of Daddy, all the toys, all the food, all the space.[1]

2. The scarcity mentality, which is present in every child at birth, is often fanned into an even hotter flame by parents who may be well meaning but who have the uncanny ability to make at least three major mistakes:

- Playing favorites.
- Comparing one sibling to another.
- Trying to be perfectly fair and equal about everything.

As we shall see in this chapter, this deadly trio of errors almost guarantees that you will have sibling rivalry. All three of these major mistakes cause more competition and jealousy among siblings and a lot less security. In short, they invite and help create the Cain and Abel syndrome. Let's take a closer look at each of these three mistakes so you can learn how to avoid them in rearing your own children.

Playing Favorites

In private counseling sessions or public seminars I often ask parents if they think they show favoritism to one of their children over another. Almost always parents will shake their heads. "Why, of course not!" seems to be written all over their faces. Unfortunately, parents do show favoritism but usually in subtle ways that they are not even aware of.

For example, you can show favoritism in the amount of time you give to one child over another. Time is a four-letter word that also spells *love*, and when we give one child a disproportionate amount of time, it creates feelings of jealousy and competition among other children in the family. The fact is, time is one expression of our priorities, and if one or more children think they are missing out, the scarcity mentality goes into overdrive.

Time is a four-letter word that also spells love.

If the truth be told, however, it is often easier to spend time with one child than another because some children are just plain difficult. Or a parent may have a simple personality clash with a certain child. On the other hand, another child is more agreeable, more interesting, or more fun.

So, it's easy to start spending more time with Susie while you leave Mary out of things, not deliberately, of course, but you just happen to be around to talk with Susie more. Or you wait for times when Mary is busy with something else and you spend the extra moments with Susie.

Another subtle way to show favoritism is nonverbally—not with your words but with your expressions. A warm look of approval for one sibling and a frown or a scowl for another is an obvious but often overlooked way that we show favoritism. Or perhaps it is in the way you use your hands or arms. For one child you open your arms or reach out to touch or pat a shoulder while another child sees your arms folded or your fingers clasped—and he or she feels rejected.

Favoritism can be shown in something as simple as the kind of questions you ask—or don't ask. As a parent, when I'm more interested in what one of my children is working on or talking about, I find myself asking more probing and interesting questions. In fact, my children often tell me to back off, because I ask too many questions about what they are doing.

Still another subtle way to show favoritism is through the words you use and your tone of voice. I counseled one family where the mother literally said things to her daughter, such as, "Honey, that's really a great job and you should really be proud of yourself that you worked so hard at school." Then in the next breath she would turn to her son and her face would change from bright to sour as she took on a directive and authoritarian tone saying, "Bob, I've told you three times to get your room cleaned up. Why don't you ever do what I ask? I getting tired of having to remind you six times a day."

When I pointed out to the mother the distinct difference in how she talked to her children, at first she was indignant. But as we talked she admitted, "I guess I find it easier to encourage Amanda because we get along so well. It's easier to criticize Bob because he and I are so different and we often disagree over lots of things."

The tone of voice and the words we use are perhaps two of the most telltale signs of how we play favorites. A typical scene finds one child misbehaving, which really irritates the parent who comes down hard with plenty of scolding and maybe even a swat or two. But another sibling can misbehave and the same parent overlooks what's happening or brushes it off with a friendly, "You think you're cute, don't you?" kind of remark. The truth is, the parent does find the other child cuter or more personable, and that's why he or she tends to be more lax in discipline or, as the parent would probably put it, "more understanding."

Breaking the Cycle. One of the most damaging things that playing favorites does is create a triangle between a parent and at least two of the children. Each sibling measures his or her worth according to the favoritism shown (or not shown) by Mom or Dad.

In the Jones family, Mom clearly favors her twelve-year-old daughter, Barb, over her ten-year-old daughter, Samantha. Barb is pretty, gets good grades in school, has lots of friends, and is cooperative at home, always willing to take responsibility and follow through. All of this is very consistent with Mom's set of personal values and her own concern about looking good in front of others and having plenty of friends. Ten-year-old Samantha, however, is average looking with a big, almost rawboned build that helps her be a good athlete, but she has few friends. In fact, Samantha tends to be a loner.

Mom is always telling Barb, "Good job" or "Thank you, Honey" or "I'm so proud of you" or "You're a joy to have as a daughter." To Samantha, however, Mom will typically say, "You should study harder and not be so wrapped up in sports." Mom shows little interest in Samantha's athletic prowess and seldom comes to see any of her softball or basketball games. Instead, she keeps harping at her to "get out and make more friends."

As this little drama is played out daily in their home, Mom, Barb, and Samantha are in a triangle where Samantha is not treated equally. Samantha is a very discouraged child who will eventually rebel against her mom in one way or another. There is a strong possibility Samantha will give up her interest in sports because it doesn't get her any recognition, only unfavorable comparisons with her sister, Barb.

Very little of this is Barb's doing. While she basks in the encouragement and interest that her mother shows to her, Barb does not give her younger sister a bad time. Nonetheless, Samantha's feelings of anger, resentment, and jealousy toward Barb will only grow. And it doesn't help any that Dad is usually working late and seldom can be there to see any of her games either.

Mom is the core of the problem. She needs to break this cycle of favoritism by encouraging each daughter to develop her own unique personality. She must recognize that each child has equal worth and value. Then she needs to encourage each child differently, but in ways that help each child feel secure as a worthwhile person.

If the cycle isn't broken, Samantha and Barb will grow up to be adult sibling rivals like so many others I have met and counseled. There may be a day when Barb will wonder why Samantha has moved away from her, doesn't contact her, and doesn't show any interest in getting together.

Barb may wind up complaining, "I don't understand why Samantha doesn't want to spend time with me. I've done nothing to hurt her. But it seems as if anything I say sets her off. I just don't understand why we can't get along better." The simple truth is that they can't get along better because the seeds of jealousy and hostility were sown years before by a mother who definitely played favorites.

Granted, this is an extreme example where you would think the mother would have become aware of what she was doing. Sad to say, though, many parents clearly play favorites this blatantly without recognizing it. What is even more common, however, is the playing of favorites on a more subtle basis. Mom may encourage one child somewhat, but there will be a subtle difference—more warmth of voice, a bit more enthusiasm—when she encourages another. Dad may try to get to activities for both children, but he is more likely to always be there when a certain child is playing or performing.

Subtle nuances in feeling and attitude are hard to detect, but they are there just the same. Parents usually do their best not to play favorites, but with one child their enthusiasm and warmth is more natural and believable, while with the other it is more forced, not quite as genuine.

And while parents may not see the difference, the children do, and they remember. This is a big reason why parents are shocked years later to hear one of their adult children say, "You always liked Judy best. She was always the favorite."

How guilty are you of showing favoritism to one child over another? To find out, take the following brief quiz and *be honest.* Your answers may reveal the need to make some changes in how you parent.

Do You Play Favorites?

True   False

____   ____   1. I am aware that I spend a disproportionate amount of time with one child compared to another.

____   ____   2. I ask questions of all my children with the same interest and curiosity.

____   ____   3. My children's interests and activities are of equal priority to me.

_____ _____ 4. I give all of my children adequate amounts of encouragement.

_____ _____ 5. I use a tone of voice that is friendly and understanding toward all of my children.

_____ _____ 6. I am aware of what each of my children is thinking and feeling.

COMPARING ONE SIBLING TO ANOTHER

When it comes to creating sibling rivals, the practice of comparing is the twin brother of favoritism. Both of these mistakes create an environment that encourages unfair and destructive competition between siblings. Many parents are well aware of the destructive nature of discouraging comparisons, such as, "Marge, why can't you be as neat as your sister?" or "Billy, if you studied half as hard as your brother, you'd be pulling A's and B's." But while these parents may scrupulously avoid the obvious kind of comparing, they may not be aware of how they compare their children in other ways that are equally and in some cases even more damaging.

In fact, many parents make certain comparisons between their children and actually think they are encouraging them when they do it! For example, a mother may say to her daughter, "When you take music lessons, I'm sure you'll do even better than your sister did at that age." Or perhaps Dad will tell his son, "You know, when Bob was your age, he couldn't do the things with a basketball that you can do."

What is wrong with the above remarks? After all, the comparison is favorable and the child is actually being complimented, not criticized. But let's look again to see what is really happening. In both cases, the parent has told the child whatever the child does in life is to be judged on a scale of _what an older sibling has done._

The girl who has been told that she's probably going to do better than her sister may be thinking, _But what if I'm not as good? I'll be a failure!_ The boy who just heard that he shows more promise in basketball than his older brother may be thinking, _Yes, but at least Bob made the varsity when he got to high school. What if I don't make the varsity? Then what?_

In both cases, the younger child is left with possible self-doubt and pressure to perform. In addition, the seeds of adult sibling rivalry are sewn, and if the younger child does not perform as well as the older sibling (or even if the younger child is successful) all kinds of feelings of rivalry and competition can come out sooner or later.

A Subtle Difference. Am I saying that parents shouldn't encourage their children at all? Far from it. We Adlerian counselors are very big on encouragement. In fact, we urge parents to *encourage* their children rather than *praise* them.

Praise ties the child's worth and value to the child's performance. . . . Encouragement . . . to his or her being.

"What's the matter with praising your kids?" parents want to know. "Isn't that the way to make them feel good about themselves?" Not necessarily. While the difference between praise and encouragement is subtle, it is still there. Praise ties the child's worth and value to the child's performance. He or she is "loved for what he can do." Encouragement ties the child's worth and value to his or her being. To put it another way, praise is usually tied to conditional love while encouragement shows unconditional love.

For example, a father comes up to his son after he pitches a no-hitter for his Little League team and says, "Great game! You're the best! I'm really proud of you!" How could this father have said something encouraging instead of simply praising his son's performance? He could say, "You really looked good today. All that practice and now a no-hitter! I'll bet that makes you feel special." (For more ideas on how to encourage your child, see the box on page 201.)

It's also a good idea not to compliment one child in front of another. Suppose, for instance, you are attending your older daughter's piano recital and your younger daughter, who is also starting to take piano, is sitting next to you. As we've already seen, you definitely don't want to say something like, "I'll bet you'll play that well some day." But you may think it would be perfectly acceptable to tell little Lori, "Isn't Lisa doing a great job?" As Faber and Mazlish point out, "Children often experience praise of a brother or sister as a put-down of themselves

. . . it's a good idea to save our enthusiastic comments for the ear of the deserving child."[2]

Granted, sometimes you get into situations where both children are present and one tells you about something special that happened at school or another is excitedly relating how he or she helped win the game. At a time like this, the way to keep feelings of rivalry at a minimum is to encourage the child who has achieved something by saying, "You must really be proud!" or "Wow! All that hard work has really paid off." Remarks like these recognize the child's achievements while not putting that child ahead of or above his or her sibling.

Ways to Encourage Your Children

There is often a subtle difference between praising and encouraging your children. When you *praise* your children, you imply or suggest that your love or acceptance depends on their "being good," or some other condition that they know pleases you. Following are a dozen phrases you can use to *encourage* your children instead. These statements focus on making the children feel good about themselves as you help them recognize their own efforts or accomplishments.

1. "You're doing a good job!"
2. "It's a pleasure to teach you when you work like that."
3. "You are really learning a lot."
4. "One more time and you'll have it."
5. "You must have been practicing."
6. "You figured that out fast."
7. "You are doing first-class work."
8. "I'm happy to see you like working at this."
9. "You are learning fast."
10. "You haven't missed a thing."
11. "You certainly did well today, don't you think?"
12. "You have made excellent progress."

Keeping Competition out of the Family. Although competition is one of the little tin gods of American culture, it is definitely a two-edged sword. Often I talk with parents, especially dads, who say, "A little competition is good for everyone, don't you think?" These same dads often coach Little League or other sports their children are involved in. Their question is logical. Isn't a little good, clean competition a good thing? After all, our society, especially our economy, is based on competition that helps create better products at better prices. It is fair to say that at the very heart of the success of American capitalism is the competition that has been the foundation of much of the greatness of our country. But where does that leave us concerning competition between siblings?

While competition is a reality in the business world, at school, and surely in the sports world, it is not something that is healthy in the family setting. It might be fair to say that *the family is the one setting where competition should not be allowed.* The family should be a shelter of unconditional acceptance, mutual support, and encouragement.

Some parents might protest that children need some competition at home to prepare them to hold their own out there in the big, bad world. I agree with Faber and Mazlish, who say that if holding your own means being able to function competently, assert yourself, and achieve your goals, "all that can be learned in an environment that encourages cooperation"[3] rather than competition.

TRYING TO BE PERFECTLY FAIR

"That's not fair!"

What parent has not heard this indignant cry of outrage from his or her children at least six times a day? (On some days it seems like sixty.) As siblings scramble to protect their turf, get their piece of the pie, and carve their own niche in the world, fairness is a big, big issue. Recognizing this, most parents bend over backward to be sure they are being "perfectly fair" in their treatment of their children.

Unfortunately, parents are fighting a losing battle when they seek to be perfectly fair because it is impossible. And ironically, the fairer parents try to be, the more sibling rivalry they can create. Even if the parent thinks that what he or she has done is fair or equal, one (or both) children will

Parents are fighting a losing battle when they seek to be perfectly fair.

not. You can count on it. There are good reasons why parents should stop trying to be perfectly fair.

For one thing, *life isn't fair.* When we try to treat our children fairly, we send them the wrong message. In reality, we need to be teaching our children that life isn't fair at all. People do get sick; people do lose their jobs or their health. Homes burn down; while some people starve, others have plenty to eat.

When you encourage your children to think that they can be treated with perfect fairness, they quickly learn that the world doesn't work that way. (They also quickly learn that they don't treat each other that way.) Instead of basking in the warm rays of fairness, they are soon shivering in the cold winds of discouragement. One child is positive that the other siblings are getting treated better than he or she is. Not only does this child become discouraged, but sibling rivalry is bound to increase.

One simple example of how this works is a typical scene where Mom serves her two children bowls of chocolate ice cream for dessert.

"There," says Mom enthusiastically. "Your favorite dessert. Bon appetit!"

Little Heather eyes Billy's bowl of ice cream then looks back at hers. She looks at both bowls from all angles and announces petulantly, "Billy's got more ice cream than I have and that's not fair!"

Horrified, Mom jumps in to attempt to right this heinous wrong: "Oh, you may be right. Let me take a little bit of Billy's and give it to you so you'll both have the same amount."

Bad idea. Billy is not happy at all with having some of his ice cream removed, and he protests, "No, you took too much and now she's got more than I have. That's not fair!"

At this point Mom decides fairness has gone far enough and she tells them both, "Be quiet! Eat your ice cream and don't complain or you'll wind up with none at all!"

Heather and Billy eat their ice cream in silence, both feeling that Mom hasn't been fair. Their big dessert treat has turned into another battleground for sibling rivalry.

How could Mom have dealt with this classic problem in a more effective way? Let's go back to Heather's first protest. Mom could have responded, "Well, Honey, you have a very good eye to tell the difference between two scoops of ice cream. Tell you what, if you're still hungry after you've finished your bowl, there's still some ice cream left in the carton in the freezer and you can have a little more."

With this approach, Mom is not being trapped into trying to be perfectly fair. She acknowledges that the child may be right—perhaps Billy's bowl of ice cream is a tad larger, but at the same time she isn't reducing Billy's bowl and she's keeping the focus clearly on the need or desire of each child and away from wrangling over who "got the most."

Granted, an obvious problem with this approach is that the minute Mom tells Heather she can have more ice cream, Billy may announce he'll want more ice cream too! Both kids could keep this dance going until they had eaten all the ice cream in the freezer!

Focusing on the child's need or desire is still a good idea, however, because it communicates that you want both children to be satisfied. If they run out of ice cream somewhere along the way, they can usually work out this conflict between themselves (more on this in Chapter 13).

Don't Treat Each Child the Same. Another count against trying to be perfectly fair is that *children should not be treated the same because they are not the same.* In other words, each child is unique. The minute you try to treat your children equally, you start to ignore or neglect each child's uniqueness. Trying to be perfectly fair covers life with a certain sameness or blandness, and it misses the true meaning of training up a child in the way he or she should go—according to his or her individual personality traits.

In our own home, my middle child, Andrea, has a wonderfully sensitive spirit. She loves animals and cares even more about people. She's a great friend, and a great help around the house—in short, Andrea is a lot of fun to be around. Naturally enough, Andrea sometimes gets in hassles with her siblings about what is fair or unfair. When dealing with Andrea, we take her sensitivity into account and try to help her see that her brothers often don't mean any harm, but they simply like to tease.

On the other hand, D.J., the baby of our family, spends much of his time alone, creating inventions or thinking about taking a trip into outer space. D.J. needs eyeball-to-eyeball communication that can bring him back down to earth. If he has misbehaved in any way, as he "fights for his rights" he needs to be made aware about the specific consequences for certain behaviors.

Evan, our first-born, is well on his way to adolescence. I try to listen to all of my children, but when Evan questions something as unfair, I am particularly concerned about hearing him out so I can fulfill his teenage desire to be treated as an adult, not a child. And I'm also careful to recognize Evan's first-born status and grant him privileges the other children don't necessarily get— for example, staying up late.

If Donna and I tried to deal with our three children fairly and equally, we would be forcing them into the same mold. Obviously, they are not of the same mold, and in trying to be perfectly fair our discipline of them could only create more competition. We try to know each of our children as well as possible and train each one in the way he or she should go according to each child's temperament and personality. We are not raising a mob; we are raising individuals.

Treating each of your children as a unique individual is one of the best ways to avoid making the three mistakes discussed in this chapter. Instead of playing favorites, making comparisons, or trying to be perfectly fair, make it your goal to encourage and bless each child according to his or her individual needs. In an earlier chapter, I mentioned the fine book, *The Gift of the Blessing*, which describes five ways to bless your children. Authors John Trent and Gary Smalley define the family blessing as beginning "with *meaningful touching*. It continues with a *spoken message* of *high value*, a message that pictures *a special future* for the individual being blessed and one that is based on an *active commitment* to see the blessing come to pass."[4]

Blessing Your Children. Even though I'm a so-called expert in child-rearing, I'm well aware that there are times when I slip up. Without meaning to or even realizing it, I play favorites (or at least my kids think I do). At other times, I may make comparisons, and I also catch myself feeling twinges of guilt when one child protests that I haven't been "perfectly fair."

To counter all these human foibles, I do my best to convey individual blessings to my children as often as possible. The family blessing, you see, isn't something that's done officially, once and for all and then it's taken care of. The family blessing is something that's done constantly, mainly through touching and talking.

On different occasions, I've taken each of our children aside to say that I recognize his or her unique interests, emotional makeup, and spiritual development. I tell this child I love him or her as a unique individual. "I picture God using you in a very special way in the years ahead," I say.

In giving each child an individual blessing, I try to point out unique characteristics—D.J.'s artistic creativity, Andrea's strong desire to be helpful, and Evan's strong sensitivity for handicapped people. I will say to Andrea, for example, "I want you to know that whatever you decide to do when you grow up, Mom and I will be praying for you and standing behind you, encouraging you every step of the way."

You can come up with your own blessing for your children, tailored to their characteristics, personalities, and needs. The important thing is to let them know that they're OK *just the way they are*, that you love them unconditionally, and that you want what is best for them.

As Faber and Mazlish put it, "Children don't need to be treated equally. They need to be treated uniquely."[5] Ironically, when parents try to be perfectly fair, they usually end up getting overly involved in their children's lives. Because all children are attention-getters, they want to get their parents involved in what they're doing or what they're thinking about. Obviously, parents do want to show interest in their children and be involved to a certain extent, but when kids start to fight, argue, and squabble, it is not the time for Mom or Dad to get totally enmeshed in their disagreement.

On our "Parent Talk" program, we have a saying that we

often share with parents who are obviously being sucked into being too involved in their children's lives. "Don't raise your sails into your child's wind." In other words, when your children huff and puff and want you to settle their disagreements and fights, you are not to "raise your sails," so to speak, and get right in the middle of the fray to settle things.

Helping your children learn to deal with conflict is a major task for all parents. How do you really handle kids who are not just bickering, but who are in a knock-down-drag-out fight? How do you bring armistice when war is raging? Not only does it take courage and patience to help your siblings learn to settle their own disputes, but it takes wisdom and some specific tools and techniques. In the next chapter we'll examine the nature of conflict and how parents can help their children learn how to deal with their conflicts themselves.

Chapter 13

HELPING YOUR CHILDREN LEARN TO DEAL WITH CONFLICT

While sibling rivalry has many faces, perhaps the biggest concern for parents centers around their children's constant bickering and fighting. Moms, especially, call into our "Parent Talk" broadcast from all points on the compass saying things like:

- "I'm at my wit's end. How can I get them to stop fighting?"

- "I'm really afraid the older one is going to hurt the younger one. What can I do?"

- "It seems that all I do is play cop. Is there any way to avoid all this constant hassle?"

"Constant hassle" is an apt description. For some parents it seems that every day is punctuated by name-calling, tattling, pinches, screams, and tears. Every night they go to bed feeling frustrated, inadequate, and guilty. There is no perfect and final answer to this perpetual problem, but there is a tool you can use to cut it down to size. This tool is what my "Parent Talk" colleague, Kevin Leman, and I call "reality discipline." Kevin actually coined this term when he wrote in the foreword of his excellent book, *Making Children Mind without Losing Yours*,

> I believe Reality Discipline is an idea whose time has come. What is Reality Discipline? Reality Discipline is a consistent, decisive, and respectful way for parents to love and discipline their children. Now notice I said "discipline" not "punish." And notice that I also said "love" and not "smother love" their children.[1]

What Dr. Leman is trying to say with this definition is that there is a middle ground between the two extreme parenting styles where so many parents fall: authoritarian and permissive. Authoritarian parents demand absolute obedience and woe to the child who disobeys. Permissive parents demand little or no obedience and literally put the child in the driver's seat.

Instead of wavering between permissiveness and authoritarianism, you need an approach that is firm but fair, what we also call "authoritative." You don't just throw up your hands in dismay and let the kids duke it out. And you don't move in like the Gestapo to "settle this thing right now." Instead, your goal is to guide your children in learning to deal with conflict themselves. What you want your kids to learn is accountability and responsibility as they make their own decisions and learn from the reality of their own mistakes and failures.

Your goal is to guide your children in learning to deal with conflict themselves.

"Sounds idyllic, Carlson," you may be muttering. "In fact, it sounds idealistic. I'd love to see my kids be more accountable and responsible—and they could start by stopping all this bickering and fighting. I'm sure other families don't have to go through this."

FAMILIES WITHOUT FRICTION

The first thing to understand is that other families do go through this, maybe more so than yours does. Conflicts between siblings are normal, and rare is the family whose siblings don't have some kind of friction and rivalry. What siblings need to learn, however, is how to resolve those conflicts in a responsible way without always running to their parents with, "Mommmm! He hit me!" or "Daaaadd! She turned off my show just as it was getting to the good part!"

A major problem, however, is that many parents grew up in homes where they didn't see healthy resolution of conflict modeled by their parents. If that's true in your case, it's very likely that you will be much more tempted to become overly involved in the "normal" fights that go on between your kids.

A mother who attended one of our "Parent Talk" seminars had an early memory of watching her parents fight. When I asked her how that memory made her feel, she said, "Nervous and scared. It's like I've become a little girl all over again and I want my parents to stop fighting."

She admitted that as an adult she gets caught up in the same emotional reaction when she catches her kids arguing and fighting. Her first thought is, *This must stop. I can't stand this confusion.*

"Let me guess," I interjected. "You jump into the fray and resolve the conflict by sending the children to their rooms." As she nodded in agreement I continued, "While this might resolve the conflict for you, it is simply repeating the sins of your parents because you aren't helping your children learn to resolve their own conflicts."

"OK, I think I understand," she said, "but how do I help them learn how to resolve their conflicts?"

I suggested three principles for doing this:

1. Always try to keep the ball in their court and not get overly involved in your children's squabbles.

2. Always be ready to take action instead of simply bawling the kids out or uttering threats like, 'You'd better
   stop, or else!'
3. Once you've taken action, stick to your guns. Don't
   let them try to draw you back into solving their problem.

You'll see these principles at work in the following examples
and discussion.

DETERMINING INTENSITY LEVELS

Let's take a closer look at the first principle in helping children learn to resolve their own conflicts: Don't get overly involved in those conflicts yourself. Notice that I said *overly* involved. I'm not saying that you don't get involved at all. There
are times when you will sit down with your children to sort out
what happened and what the real problem is (more on that
later), but your first goal is to keep the ball in their court as
much as you possibly can. Only then will they learn how to play
the conflict-resolution game.

It's important to note the level of intensity when your kids are
arguing or fighting. In dealing with my own children, I desig-
nate three levels of intensity with the colors blue, yellow, and
red.

Blue Zone: Everyday Bickering. The blue level involves
the everyday bickering and arguing that goes on with all siblings. As much as possible, I try to stay out of this unless it
breaks a specific family rule, such as no name-calling. When I
start hearing terms like "Dork!" "Jerk!" or worse, I move in to
remind the kids of reality. While it's OK for siblings to send I-
messages telling each other how they feel, it is not OK to assassi-
nate each other's character. When the language starts to become
abusive, siblings are moving out of the blue zone and into the
yellow zone, which means that you need to intervene.

Yellow Zone: Situation Heating Up. The yellow level of
intensity finds the situation definitely heating up. A typical

run-in finds kids arguing over a toy or accusing each other of hitting, pushing, or pinching. Their anger level hasn't escalated to the red zone, but it's on the way. Now the children need guidance that will set them up to resolve their conflict on their own.

As you step into the fray, acknowledge that you can see that both of your children are angry. Say something like, "Wow, it sounds as if you two are really upset with one another. What's going on?" If your children are normal, each child will hasten to give his or her side of the situation.

Your next step is not to render a Solomon-like decision to settle the problem. Instead, let your kids know that you can see that "this is a difficult problem and it needs to be worked out." For example, suppose they're fighting over a Nintendo game and all of its delicate wires and controls are in danger of being torn asunder.

Instead of delivering a typical lecture about, "Why can't you learn to share?" try another tack. Say something like: "This one looks as if it will be hard to call. Both of you want to play Nintendo at the same time and this particular Nintendo game is only for one player at a time. Tell you what. Why don't you both leave the game here and go to another room where the two of you can figure out some way to have each person use the game for an equal amount of time? I feel confident you two kids can come up with a good solution to this problem."

Then, if necessary, take both children by the hand and guide them to another room where they can work out a schedule for using the Nintendo game. Tell them that when they have the schedule worked out to come and see you and tell you on what basis they plan to continue to play the game.

Obviously, this approach isn't foolproof. A lot depends on the ages of the children and how willing both of them are to compromise. But the advantage of this approach is that, first, it gives them an opportunity to try to resolve their own conflicts; and, second, by going through these various steps, the "payoff" in the fighting and squabbling (such as getting you involved) is greatly reduced. With any luck, the two of them are very likely to come to the obvious conclusion that each one gets to play with the game for so many minutes and then relinquishes it so the other child can have a turn rather than neither of them playing Nintendo at all. This kind of approach is what Adele Faber and Elaine Mazlish call "intervening without interfering."[2]

Helping children learn how to resolve yellow-zone conflicts doesn't mean you simply say, "You two kids work this out—I'll be in the next room reading my magazine." To intervene means to take action, but with a minimum of words. Calm the situation down, then give the children directions on how they can solve their own problem. Finally, trust them enough to let them try to do just that. If they come back to you whining and complaining that the other one isn't being fair, stick to your guns and tell them nicely, "Well, you haven't been able to solve this problem yet, but I believe you can. Go back and try again."

If the children ultimately fail to come to a reasonable solution, you can always take more action and invoke logical consequences because of the reality of the situation. In other words, if they can't agree on how to play with the Nintendo, then they will both have to forego using the game for a given amount of time.

For this approach to work, you must keep your cool. It's all too easy to become angry because the kids are fighting again. They seem to have a sixth sense for knowing when to get into a yellow-zone or possibly worse conflict—just when you are trying to read your paper, watch your favorite newscast, or get some housework done.

Keep in mind also that many kids deliberately get into fights and squabbles just so they can watch Mom and Dad "blow their top." If you refuse to do this, a lot of the payoff for fighting is removed. That alone can solve a great many conflicts.

Danger: Red-Zone Conflict. What happens when a conflict moves well past the yellow zone into the red? Perhaps several blows have already been landed by the time you arrive. One sibling is ready to administer the coup de grace with her baseball bat while the other is brandishing his Tonka truck high above his head Godzilla-style, ready to hurl it at his foe.

This is no time for diplomatic observations. You need to take decisive, immediate action to separate the battling siblings and get them into a "cooling-off mode." The time for working it out will come later.

Suppose Dad is home and he hears the ruckus. He leaps from his recliner and bursts into the room where his children are having at it. Sizing up the situation in a flash, he orders the two combatants to "STOP!" So far so good, but then Dad asks the dumbest question any parent can ever ask kids who are fighting: "All right, *who* started it?"

Does Dad really think the culprit who started the battle is going to step forward and say, "I cannot tell a lie, Dad. I started it and I'm willing to pay the consequences"?

Instead, all Dad hears is screaming and arguing as both kids point their fingers and blame each other, talking at the same time at the top of their lungs.

Naturally, Dad can't stand for this. He steps in and tries to become judge and jury as he sorts out all the facts. That way he can dispense justice that is "perfectly fair."

Alas, Dad's attempts at playing Solomon are doomed because both children feel they are not to blame. Whoever Dad finally finds guilty is going to feel that he or she wasn't treated fairly. In fact, as Dad sends the older child off to his or her room (it's always the older child who's guilty; just ask the younger one), the last thing Dad will hear before the slamming of the door is, "That's not fair! You always blame me and let him (or her) get away with murder!"

Dad sighs and returns to his paper, sure that he has done all that he can to judge fairly and keep peace in his home. Actually, he has created even more competition—and rivalry— between his children. In trying to sort out, "Who started it?" he put himself in an absolute no-win situation. What could he have done to handle the situation more effectively?

For one thing, Dad should have been aware that his job is not to treat his children fairly, but to teach them about living life. After he stepped in and stopped the battle, he should have taken both boys by the hand and said, "I see that you are really upset and want to hurt each other. We can't have that so it's time-out until we can all cool down."

Then Dad should have left each boy in a separate room where they could have time to think about what happened and realize there might be better ways to settle differences than with name-calling and hitting.

It takes two to tangle. When siblings can't settle an argument themselves . . . they need some help in resolving their conflict.

Would both boys agree that taking a time out was a good and fair solution? Probably not. At this point, Dad must simply keep a smile on his face and stick to his guns. Training children is an ongoing process. It takes time, repetition of principles, and patience—a *lot* of patience. Instead of being sucked into arguments, Dad can simply say, "I'm really not concerned about whose fault it was. First you go cool down and *then* we'll talk about what happened."

Parents should always remember that fighting is really an act of cooperation between two siblings. In other words, it takes two to tangle. When siblings can't settle an argument themselves they move out of the yellow zone and into the red zone, where they need some help in resolving their conflict.

A THREE-STEP PLAN FOR CONFLICT RESOLUTION

After a suitable amount of time, call the children back together to sort out what happened. This would also be a good time to suggest that they both apologize to one another. With younger children, this may be enough. With older children, age ten or above, there may be an ongoing problem that has been causing the fighting. If you think this is true, you may find the following "conflict-resolution model" useful:

1. Ask "What's the Real Problem?" Sit the children down and ask them this question. Naturally each child will say it is his or her sibling who is the real problem. Give each child a chance to talk without being interrupted by the other as you sort out who is angry, who is hurt, who thinks he or she is being picked on, and who thinks something is unfair. Make no judgments on this input. Simply try to identify what the real problem is.

2. Ask each child to describe what part he or she is playing in causing the conflict. Granted, many children, particularly younger kids, will be quite sure they aren't playing any part in causing the problem. It's all their sibling's fault, they will say. When children are a bit older, however, and you have them in a setting where their anger is cooled and the whole conflict has been de-escalated, you can get them to start thinking about exactly what they're doing to cause the fighting.

3. Ask each child, "What are you willing to do to solve this problem?" This is the most important question of all. It asks each child to come up with some ideas about how he or she will change, or it forces the child to offer solutions he or she is willing to live with. At this point, it's a good idea to write down some rules that both children can agree upon. In fact, encourage the children to contribute freely. Kids love to spell out ground rules because in their hearts all children are budding lawyers who want to be treated fairly.

Once you have some rules spelled out that everyone believes he or she can live with, give the children a chance to follow them. See how it goes for a few days or maybe a week. Then call them back together to report on what's been happening and how well the new arrangement is working.

RESOLVING CONFLICT BETWEEN A SLOB AND NEATNIK

For an example of how this conflict-resolution model can work, suppose we have two girls ages ten and twelve, who have to share the same bedroom. They argue over almost everything: closet space, who is being messy, who is too noisy, and who took whose new sweater. Mom is constantly being called on to settle their disputes.

One day, after finding the girls almost ready to come to blows, she lets them cool off in separate rooms and then calls them together for a conflict-resolution session. Nancy, the oldest, goes first by describing what she believes is the real problem: "Becky is a slob," she says vehemently. "She leaves her clothes lying all over the room, she spills milk and graham crackers on my desk, and she's always stealing my clothes!"

Now it's Becky's turn: "Nancy is too fussy. She screams if any little thing is out of place and I only spilled milk and graham crackers once. As for stealing clothes, I borrowed a sweater a couple of times, but I don't know why she's so upset about that."

"So how do each of you think you are contributing to the problem?" Mom asks. As she guides her daughters into identifying the problem, she helps them see they have different standards. Each has unrealistic expectations of the other. Each girl is thinking, *Why can't she be just like me?*

Becky is obviously a messy free spirit who doesn't put much value on keeping her belongings in perfect order. Nancy values neatness and perfection a great deal—so much so that she is judgmental and at times unreasonable—a particularly difficult combination for a messy sibling to live with. If the girls don't learn to resolve their differences now, they may experience much more severe rivalry as they grow older and become adults. The Cain and Able syndrome is often spawned among widely differing values that cause such severe differences neither sibling can respect the other.

Finally, Mom asks both girls what they can do to solve their problem. At this point, she helps them spell out some ground rules for living together in their room that they both agree upon. What often works in a situation like this is to get the girls to recognize whose side of the room is whose. The "slob" has the right to be sloppy, but only on her side of the room. She can't spill over onto her neatnik sister's side.

At the same time, Nancy the neatnik cannot be constantly harping at and criticizing her sister for being sloppy. It's Becky's prerogative to be messy as long as it's on her side of the room. As for spilling food on desks, the girls may decide that the best solution is not to bring food into the room at all.

Borrowing clothes is another tough one, but by the time the sisters get through negotiating they may agree that borrowing clothes might work as long as the one who wants to borrow asks the other one if it's OK.

Once all the rules are spelled out, Mom can turn them loose to see how they will live together with their new arrangement. But she has to be firm about one thing: She will not referee their squabbles. They will have to use their new rules and settle their disputes between themselves. If they can't settle their disagreements themselves, both of them will have to pay the consequences on an equal basis. No one will get off the hook by claiming, "It's her fault!"

THE GOAL OF GOOD PARENTING

In these final chapters, I have tried to give some basic principles to help you guide your children away from the Cain and Abel syndrome—continuing sibling rivalry that becomes increasingly bitter and hostile. Many excellent tools are available to assist you with this (see the list of recommended reading in the box on page 221), but perhaps some of the most practical advice I ever heard came from Dr. Charles Swindoll, the widely known pastor of the Evangelical Free Church of Fullerton, California, and author of more than thirty books, many of them best-sellers.

Chuck was our guest on "Parent Talk" one day, and during the interview he commented that his four children, who are now married with families of their own, all get along well together and love to be with each other and their parents. When we asked Chuck how he and his wife, Cynthia, dealt with their kids when they got into childhood battles, he made the following observation:

Cynthia was wonderful at handling that. We took time not to let them fight. We didn't believe they could solve anything with their fists. We told them God gave them a mouth and two ears, and to keep their hands in their pockets and talk it out and listen to one another. They had to stay at it until they got the thing resolved.

We tried our best not to prejudge what the problem was, but to let our kids tell us. It all starts with truth. You teach your kids to tell the truth. If the kids lie, you don't have the information you need and you never know if you're working with facts or not. So we would always emphasize that it was safe to tell us the truth, and in the long run it was always best to tell the truth.

On the basis of the truth, we would work out what the

problem was, and when it was necessary we would point out where someone was wrong and needed to make an apology.

But we never forced our children to apologize to each other. We never forced "I'm sorry" out of anybody, because God doesn't force it out of us. We always let the kids come to terms with the situation and then apologize because they wanted to.

Today Chuck and Cynthia are grandparents who are still successfully battling the Cain and Abel syndrome in the next generation. Two days before joining us on "Parent Talk," Chuck had been home alone with his grandchildren, Parker, age five, and Heather, age three. Parker socked Heather, and when Grandpa Swindoll asked him why, he said, "I don't like her. She's dumb. She aggravates me."

All Heather could say was, "Yes, yes! He hit me! He hit me!"

Grandpa tried to get them both calmed down and to find out why Parker had hit his sister. As it turned out, she had aggravated him. Yes, he was wrong to hit her, but she shouldn't have teased him, something she does quite often.

When Grandpa asked Parker how he felt, he said, "I feel mad."

Grandpa knew that this was not the time to ask Parker to say he was sorry. Instead he said, "OK, Parker. Heather and I are going out back on the sun porch, and you can stay here and think about it. When you want to talk to Heather, you let me know."

A long time passed—to Grandpa it seemed very long. Finally Parker called out, "Bubba, I want to talk to her." So Grandpa brought the children together and Parker looked at his sister and said, "Sorry."

Grandpa told Parker to wait a minute, that saying "Sorry" was a start, but what was he sorry about?

"Sorry I hit you," said Parker, wanting to get it over with.

But Grandpa didn't let it stop there. He urged Parker to talk about it with his little sister. And in those next brief moments the children got experience, at their preschool level, in how to talk things through. It wasn't long, however, before Heather said, "I'm tried of talking about this. Let's go play."

"So they got it all worked out," Chuck said. "I know it isn't always that simple, but I still think that when kids learn to tell the truth and they know that Mom or Dad or Grandma or Grandpa aren't going to play favorites, then you've got a lot going for you. You're on your way to working it out."

In the long run our goal is to raise adults, not children.

Dr. Swindoll's words are worth pondering by all of us who have one of the toughest jobs on the face of the earth—parenting. Some days can be discouraging, but it helps to remember that in the long run our goal is to raise adults, not children. Our job as parents is to prepare each of our kids to face the real world and to teach them the spiritual values that will not fail them when the going gets tough.

And the going *will* get tough. No matter how hard you work at parenting, it won't guarantee that your children will grow up to be best friends. As your children grow and leave home, it is inevitable that they will have differences—different professions, different interests, different educations, different spouses, different lives. Because of all these factors, which will be out of your control when they are grown and gone, you must do what you can now to neutralize the effects of the Cain and Abel syndrome.

Your home is a training ground for the future. In the safety of the family circle, children can learn to negotiate differences; to make good choices; and to accept, respect, and even love one another. The cycle can be broken if you follow basic rules like these each day:

- Teach your kids to tell the truth and always be truthful with them.
- Teach your kids to respect each other by modeling respect for your spouse and everyone else in the family.
- Never play favorites; do your best to convince each of your children that he or she is "the favorite."
- Keep your cool and your sense of humor.
- And above all else, never, never give up!

Recommended Tools for Combating the Cain and Abel Syndrome

Siblings without Rivalry by Adele Faber and Elaine Mazlish (Avon Books, 1998). How to help your children live together so you can live with them too.

Parent Talk by Dr. Kevin Leman and Randy Carlson (Thomas Nelson Publishers, 1993). Straight answers to the questions that rattle moms and dads.

Making Children Mind without Losing Yours by Dr. Kevin Leman (Dell Publishing, reprinted by arrangement with Fleming H. Revell Company, 1987). How to use reality discipline to raise responsible kids.

Smart Kids, Stupid Choices by Dr. Kevin Leman (Regal Books, 1987). A survival guide for parents of teenagers.

Epilogue

The Power of the Magic Eyes

As I worked on the final draft of this book, I lay flat on my back recuperating from a gallbladder operation. I had been getting signals from my deteriorating gallbladder all summer, and one night it decided enough was enough. The pain became excruciating, and I made a 1:00 A.M. trip to the hospital. By 8:00 P.M. that same evening, my gallbladder and I parted company and we are both the better for it.

You may be wondering, Did Randy's brothers rush to Randy's bedside? No, they did not, which is perfectly OK with me. Gallbladder operations are seldom life-threatening, and round-trip plane flights from Michigan to Arizona are time-consuming and expensive. Both of them telephoned, however, the day after my surgery to express their concern and wish me well. Larry seemed particularly sympathetic and made it a point to say he wished he could be in town and able to drop by the hospital.

When Warren called, he spoke with empathy, having had his own gallbladder removed just two years before. We spent quite a while talking about the new and improved techniques. His had been the old-fashioned "split-you-open-and-lift-it-out" method, while I had benefited from the "four-small-incisions-and-pull-it-through" approach that was supposed to shorten recuperation time by several weeks.

Neither call was full of warm fuzzies. The Carlsons aren't known for being expressively affectionate. What Larry and Warren said to me was about what I would have said to them had our positions been reversed. Nonetheless, those conversations with my brothers did much to lift my spirits.

Before either call came in, I had been telling myself, *A gallbladder operation is no big deal. Larry or Warren may be out of town or too busy to call, but that will still be OK with me.*

But I knew I was kidding myself. A gallbladder operation *is* a big enough deal and I was *glad* when they telephoned. My big brothers *did* care. When the chips were down, they were right there rooting for little Fat Butt to come through OK, and it made me feel good.

Here, in the midst of our own Carlson sibling moment, was a simple but potent demonstration of the power of siblinghood. As Jane Greer puts it, being a sibling "has the potential for filling our lives with delight, amusement, reassurance, and consolation; anger, bafflement, and exasperation; companionship or loneliness; the warmest friendship or the coldest enmity. For most people, siblinghood is a mix of experiences, some of which can create both internal and external conflict."[1]

I know, as only a sibling can know, how true that is. And as I look back to sort out the years, I realize that being the little brother of Warren and Larry has been a real mix of experiences. They haven't all been good, but they certainly haven't all been bad either. My brothers haven't *always* teased and tormented me; nor have they *always* ignored and discounted me.

One of the most effective counseling tools I use is helping clients explore their early-childhood memories. What we remember on a consistent basis and how we feel about those consistent memories tell us a great deal about ourselves today. But beyond that, we gain insight into how we can change our attitudes and behavior to become better-functioning persons as well as well-connected siblings who do not fall victim to the Cain and Abel syndrome.

Now at the age of forty-one, minus my gallbladder and vowing anew to stop working too hard and start saying no a little more often, I am more aware than ever that keeping up sibling ties is far more important than nursing hurts from the past. The past is always a tangle of goods and bads, negatives and positives, pros and cons. As we sort it all out, we can appreciate the ways we have changed while recognizing the ways we have remained the same.

As I lay there doing my best not to cough or laugh too hard, I thought of a visit I made to Michigan years after I had married and had moved west to Arizona. As I drove down the old street where I had grown up as a boy, I could still remember the day the neighborhood bully had tried to push me around and how Larry had "cleaned his clock." And as I came up to the house that had been ours I could almost see Warren out in the driveway, washing his 1957 Ford, a really "mean machine" in which he often gave me rides.

I parked in front and sat there looking at the old place for a few minutes as the memories came flooding back. That picket fence that Larry built still stood strong and sound, and the mounting brackets that had held Warren's ham radio antenna were still on the roof. Just a few blocks away was the same little church where I had, at age eleven, served as an usher in Warren's wedding. I could still remember the warm glow of pride I felt when Warren asked me to be part of one of the most important days of his life.

Several families have owned that home since we lived there during the sixties, but it's still a point of reference for me. It's where I grew up with my big brothers. It's where I "came from." And as I sat there remembering, the good memories were predominant.

What is the secret to being able to sort out the good and leave the bad buried in the past? It's clear enough that, as my brothers and I grow older, the advantages of being closer as siblings are becoming much more apparent to all of us. There is, of course, no magic formula. Childhood labels, perceptions, and expectations all die hard, and $E - R = D$ is still an unerring equation for disappointment. In Jane Leder's words, "Despite all good intentions, a sibling's wish to forgive and understand is often greater than his or her ability to do so."[2]

Perhaps this is why Scripture speaks often of the need for divine help and direction in learning how to forgive. While our ability may sometimes be weak, our desire to forgive can overpower the hurt and pain that keep us carrying those grudges from long ago. If we ask God for help, He will give it.

In *Forgive and Forget*, author Lewis B. Smedes includes a perceptive look at forgiveness with "The Magic Eyes," the short fable that follows. Smedes said the fable came to him one night as he was writing.

In the village of Faken in innermost Friesland there lived a long thin baker named Fouke, a righteous man, with a long thin chin and a long thin nose. Fouke was so upright that he seemed to spray righteousness from his thin lips over everyone who came near him; so that people of Faken preferred to stay away.

Fouke's wife, Hilda, was short and round, her arms were round, her bosom was round, her rump was round. Hilda did not keep people at bay with righteousness; her soft roundness seemed to invite them instead to come close to her in order to share the warm cheer of her open heart.

Hilda respected her righteous husband, and loved him too, as much as he allowed her; but her heart ached for something more from him than his worthy righteousness.

And there, in the bed of her need, lay the seed of sadness.

One morning, having worked since dawn to knead his dough for the ovens, Fouke came home and found a stranger in his bedroom lying on Hilda's round bosom.

Hilda's adultery soon became the talk of the tavern and the scandal of the Faken congregation. Everyone assumed that Fouke would cast Hilda out of his house, so righteous was he. But he surprised everyone by keeping Hilda as his wife, saying he forgave her, as the Good Book said he should.

In his heart of hearts, however, Fouke could not forgive Hilda for bringing shame to his name. Whenever he thought about her, his feelings toward her were angry and hard; he despised her as if she were a common whore. When it came right down to it, he hated her for betraying him after he had been so good and so faithful a husband to her.

He only pretended to forgive Hilda so that he could punish her with his righteous mercy.

But Fouke's fakery did not sit well in heaven.

So each time that Fouke would feel his secret hate toward Hilda, an angel came to him and dropped a small pebble, hardly the size of a shirt button, into Fouke's heart. Each time a pebble dropped, Fouke would feel a stab of pain like the pain he felt the moment he came on Hilda feeding her hungry heart from a stranger's larder.

Thus he hated her the more; his hate brought him pain and his pain made him hate.

The pebbles multiplied. And Fouke's heart grew very heavy with the weight of them, so heavy that the top half of his body bent forward so far that he had to strain his neck upward in order to see straight ahead. Weary with hurt, Fouke began to wish he were dead.

The angel who dropped the pebbles into his heart came to Fouke one night and told him how he could be healed of his hurt.

"Only a new way of looking at things through the magic eyes could heal the hurt flowing from the wounds of yesterday."

There was one remedy, he said, only one, for the hurt of a wounded heart. Fouke would need the miracle of the magic eyes. He would need eyes that could look back to the beginning of his hurt and see his Hilda, not as a wife who betrayed him, but as a weak woman who needed him. Only a new way of looking at things through the magic eyes could heal the hurt flowing from the wounds of yesterday.

Fouke protested. "Nothing can change the past," he said. "Hilda is guilty, a fact that not even an angel can change."

"Yes, poor hurting man, you are right," the angel said. "You cannot change the past, you can only heal the hurt that comes to you from the past. And you can heal it only with the vision of the magic eyes."

"And how can I get your magic eyes?" pouted Fouke.

"Only ask, desiring as you ask, and they will be given you.

And each time you see Hilda through your new eyes, one pebble will be lifted from your aching heart."

Fouke could not ask at once, for he had grown to love his hatred. But the pain of his heart finally drove him to want and to ask for the magic eyes that the angel had promised. So he asked. And the angel gave.

Soon Hilda began to change in front of Fouke's eyes, wonderfully and mysteriously. He began to see her as a needy woman who loved him instead of a wicked woman who betrayed him.

The angel kept his promise; he lifted the pebbles from Fouke's heart, one by one, though it took a long time to take them all away. Fouke gradually felt his heart grow lighter; he began to walk straight again, and somehow his nose and his chin seemed less thin and sharp than before. He invited Hilda to come into his heart again, and she came, and together they began a journey into their second season of humble joy.[3]

I believe Dr. Smedes's fable has special meaning for all adult siblings. When we fail to see with the magic eyes of forgiveness, we continue to carry pain from the past, whether that pain be petty or profound. But when we look through magic eyes on our siblings and they do the same to us, the load is lifted. We can take hold of past experiences, remember what happened more fully, and understand it better. As we see causes and effects, we can reach new insights about the family dynamics that influenced us.[4] The Cain and Abel syndrome is neutralized and loving our brothers and sisters becomes not only possible but a daily reality.

Notes

Chapter 1 Does Rivalry Really Matter?

1. See Jeanne Wolf, "The Smothers Brothers: A New Life for the Old Team," *McCalls*, May 1989, 105.

2. Ibid., 105.

3. Ibid., 107.

4. Francine Klagsbrun, *Mixed Feelings* (New York: Bantam, 1992), 356.

5. Ibid., 7.

6. William Morris, ed., *The American Heritage Dictionary of the English Language* (Boston: Houghton-Mifflin, 1969), 1121.

7. Jane Greer with Edward Myers, *Adult Sibling Rivalry* (New York: Crown, 1992), 2.

8. See Stephen Covey, *Principle-Centered Leadership* (New York: Simon and Schuster, Fireside, 1990–91), 205.

9. Kevin Leman and Randy Carlson, *Unlocking the Secrets of Your Childhood Memories* (Nashville: Thomas Nelson, 1989), 14.

10. Bradford Wilson and George Edington, *First Child, Second Child . . . Your Birth Order Profile* (New York: McGraw-Hill, 1981), 5.

11. Greer and Myers, *Adult Sibling Rivalry*, 11.

Chapter 2 The Cain and Abel Syndrome

1. Robert Jamieson, A. R. Fausset, David Brown, *Commentary Practical and Explanatory on the Whole Bible* (Grand Rapids: Zondervan, 1962), 21.

2. See John Bradshaw, *Bradshaw on the Family* (Deerfield Beach, Fla.: Health Communications, 1988), chapters 3 and 4.

3. Jane Leder, *Brothers and Sisters: How They Shape Our Lives* (New York: St. Martins, 1991), 34.

4. See Leder, *Brothers and Sisters: How They Shape Our Lives*, 33–35.

5. Ibid., 261–62.

6. The Associated Press, "Sibling Abuse Leaves Long-Lasting Effects," *Jackson Citizen Patriot*, 15 Aug. 1992, B4.

Chapter 3 Batting at the Bottom of Your Birth Order

1. Klagsbrun, *Mixed Feelings*, 62–63.

2. Ibid., 97.

Chapter 4 Siblings: Players on the Family's Stage

1. Greer and Myers, *Adult Sibling Rivalry*, 19.

2. Leman and Carlson, *Unlocking the Secrets of Your Childhood Memories*, 45.

3. Greer and Myers, *Adult Sibling Rivalry*, 18–19.

4. Ibid., 19.

Chapter 5 Coming to Grips with the Green-Eyed Monster

1. The information in this chapter about the Kennedy brothers is adapted from Judy Mills, *John F. Kennedy* (New York: Franklin Watts, 1988).

2. Mills, *John F. Kennedy*, 58.

3. Ibid., 78.

4. Charles F. Pfeiffer and Everett F. Harrison, eds., *The Wycliffe Bible Commentary* (Chicago: Moody, 1962), 30.

5. The blessing of biblical times is still carried on in certain forms today among Orthodox Jewish families. See Gary Smalley and John Trent, *The Gift of the Blessing* (Nashville: Thomas Nelson, 1993), 9–10.

6. Thomas J. Watson, Jr., and Peter Petre, *Father, Son, and Company* (New York: Bantam), 173.

7. See Watson and Petre, *Father, Son, and Company*, 173–180.

Chapter 6 The Secrets to Being Close to Your Siblings

1. Barbara Mandrell with George Vecsey, *Get to the Heart* (New York: Bantam, 1990), 49, 51.

2. Ibid., 46.

3. Ibid., 47, 51.

4. Kathryn Hepburn, *Me: Stories of My Life* (New York: Alfred A. Knopf, 1991), 27, 30.

5. Tom Crouch, *The Bishop's Boys: A Life of Wilbur and Orville Wright* (New York: W. W. Norton, 1989), 13.

6. Hepburn, *Me*, 26–27.

7. Crouch, *The Bishop's Boys*, 49.

8. Ivonette Wright Miller, "Character Study," in Ivonette Miller, ed., *Wright Reminiscences* (Dayton, Ohio: privately published, 1978), 61. Quoted in Crouch, *The Bishop's Boys*, 103.

9. Wilbur Wright's Last Will and Testament, 10 May 1912, in Alfred Stokes Andrews, *The Andrews, Clap, Stokes, Wright, Van Cleve Genealo-*

gies (Ft. Lauderdale, Fla.: privately published, 1984), 512. Quoted in Crouch, *The Bishop's Boys*, 49.

10. Wilbur Wright, 3 April 1912, in Marvin W. McFarland, ed., *The Papers of Wilbur and Orville Wright*, vol. 1 (New York: McGraw-Hill, 1953), v. Quoted in Crouch, *The Bishop's Boys*, 49, 50.

11. Smalley and Trent, *The Gift of the Blessing*, 9.

12. Ibid., 19.

13. Ibid., 39.

14. Hepburn, *Me*, 30.

15. Mandrell and Vecsey, *Get to the Heart*, 52.

16. Smalley and Trent, *The Gift of the Blessing*, 107–8.

Chapter 7 Solving the Rivalry Riddle

1. Leder, *Brothers and Sisters: How They Shape Our Lives*, 228.

Chapter 8 Bridging the Gap between You and Your Siblings

1. David Augsburger, *Caring Enough to Confront* (Ventura, Calif.: Regal, 1985), 52.

2. William Backus and Marie Chapian, *Telling Yourself the Truth* (Minneapolis, Bethany Fellowship, 1980), 17.

3. Klagsbrun, *Mixed Feelings*, 164.

4. Lewis Smedes, *Forgive and Forget: Healing the Hurts We Don't Deserve* (New York: Pocket Books, a division of Simon and Schuster, 1984), 12.

5. Ibid., 126.

6. Ibid., 12.

7. David Augsburger, *Caring Enough to Forgive*, 56.

Chapter 9 Putting an End to the Eternal Triangles

1. Henry Cloud, *Changes That Heal* (Grand Rapids: Zondervan, 1990), 209.

2. Ibid., 92.

3. Klagsbrun, *Mixed Feelings*, 312.

4. Ibid., 265.

Chapter 10 When Siblings' Values Clash

1. See Benjamin Benson with Edwin Crego and Ronald Drucker, *Your Family Business: A Success Guide for Growth and Survival* (Homewood, Ill.: Business One Irwin, 1990), 50.

2. Greer and Myers, *Adult Sibling Rivalry*, 115—ed16.

3. Klagsbrun, *Mixed Feelings*, 180.

4. Leder, *Brothers and Sisters: How They Shape Our Lives*, 229.

Chapter 11 What to Do If You Hit a "Blank Wall"

1. For a helpful discussion of these four approaches to anger (expressing, repressing, suppressing, confessing) see H. Norman Wright, *Communication: Key to Your Marriage* (Ventura, Calif.: Regal, 1974), 87–93.

2. Peggy Say, "The Dream That Died," *Redbook*, December 1992, 38.

3. Ibid., 42.

4. Ibid.

Chapter 12 Avoiding the Mistakes That Creat Sibling Rivalry

1. Adele Faber and Elaine Mazlish, *Siblings without Rivalry* (New York: Avon, 1987), 15.

2. Ibid., 77–78.

3. Ibid., 77.

4. Trent and Smalley, *The Gift of the Blessing*, 18.

5. Faber and Mazlish, *Siblings without Rivalry*, 99.

Chapter 13 Helping Your Children Learn to Deal with Conflict

1. Kevin Leman, *Making Children Mind without Losing Yours* (Grand Rapids: Revell, 1984), 9.

2. Faber and Mazlish, *Siblings without Rivalry*, 147.

Epilogue: The Power of the Magic Eyes

1. Greer and Myers, *Adult Sibling Rivalry*, 215.

2. Leder, *Brothers and Sisters: How They Shape Our Lives*, 229.

3. Smedes, *Forgive and Forget*, 13–15.

4. See Greer and Myers, *Adult Sibling Rivalry*, 11.